LawExpress

CONSTITUTIONAL AND ADMINISTRATIVE LAW

Law Express

CONSTITUTIONAL AND ADMINISTRATIVE LAW

6th edition

Chris Taylor
Senior Lecturer in Law, University of Bradford

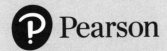 Pearson

Harlow, England • London • New York • Boston • San Francisco • Toronto • Sydney • Dubai • Singapore • Hong Kong
Tokyo • Seoul • Taipei • New Delhi • Cape Town • São Paulo • Mexico City • Madrid • Amsterdam • Munich • Paris • Milan

PEARSON EDUCATION LIMITED
KAO Two
KAO Park
Harlow CM17 9NA
United Kingdom
Tel: +44 (0)1279 623623
Web: www.pearson.com/uk

First published 2008 (print and electronic)
Second edition published 2010 (print and electronic)
Third edition published 2013 (print and electronic)
Fourth edition published 2015 (print and electronic)
Fifth edition published 2017 (print and electronic)
Sixth edition published 2019 (print and electronic)

Contains public sector information licensed under the Open Government Licence (OGL) v3.0.
http://www.nationalarchives.gov.uk/doc/open-government-licence/version/3/

Contains parliamentary information licensed under the Open Parliament Licence (OPL) v3.0.
http://www.parliament.uk/site-information/copyright/open-parliament-licence/

Pearson Education is not responsible for the content of third-party internet sites.

ISBN: 978-1-292-21010-0 (print)
978-1-292-21080-3 (PDF)
978-1-292-21062-9 (ePub)

British Library Cataloguing-in-Publication Data
A catalogue record for the print edition is available from the British Library

10 9 8 7 6 5 4 3 2 1
23 22 21 20 19 18

Print edition typeset in 10/12pt Helvetica Neue LT W1G by Spi Global
Printed and bound in Malaysia (CTP-PJB)

NOTE THAT ANY PAGE CROSS REFERENCES REFER TO THE PRINT EDITION

Contents

Acknowledgements

Our thanks go to all reviewers who contributed to the development of this text, including students who participated in research and focus groups which helped to shape the series format.

Chris Taylor
Senior Lecturer in Law
University of Bradford

Publisher's acknowledgements

We are grateful to the following for permission to reproduce copyright material:

Extract on page 23 from *BBC* v *Johns (Inspector of Taxes)* [1965] Ch 32 (CA), Lord Diplock; Extract on page 24 from *Malone* v *Metropolitan Police Commissioner (No. 2)* [1979] Ch 344 (CH), Megarry VC; Extract on page 24 from *Attorney General* v *De Keyser's Royal Hotel Ltd* [1920] AC 508 (HL), Parmoor L.; Extract on page 25 from *Gouriet* v *Union of Post Office Workers* [1978] AC 435 (HL), Viscount Dilhorne; Extract on page 26 from *Council of Civil Service Unions* v *Minister for the Civil Service (the GCHQ case)* [1985] AC 374 (HL), Lord Roskill; Extract on page 27 from *R* v *Secretary of State for the Home Department, ex parte Northumbria Police Authority* [1989] QB 26 (CA), Purchas LJ; Extract on page 27 from *R* v *Secretary of State for Foreign and Commonwealth Affairs, ex parte Everett* [1989] QB 811 (CA), O'Connor LJ; Extract on page 28 from *R* v *Secretary of State for the Home Department, ex parte Bentley* [1994] QB 349; Extract on page 28 from *R* v *Secretary of State for Foreign and Commonwealth Affairs, ex parte Rees-Mogg* [1994] QB 552, Lloyd LJ; Extract on page 40 from *M* v *Home Office* [1994] 1 AC 377, Lord Templeman; Extract on page 41 from *R* v *Secretary of State for the Home Department, ex parte Anderson* [2003] 1 AC 837, Lord Steyn; Extract on page 41 from *R* v *Secretary of State for the Home Department, ex parte Fire Bri-gades Union* [1995] 2 AC 513, Lord Browne-Wilkinson; Extract on page 44 from *Antoine* v *Sharma* [2007] 1 WLR 780, Lord Bingham; Extract on page 48 from *Vauxhall Estates Ltd* v *Liverpool Corporation* [1932] 1 KB 733 (DC), Avory J; Extract on page 48 from *British Railways Board* v *Pickin* [1974] AC 765 (HL), Lord Reid; Extract on page 50 from *R* v *Secretary of State for Transport, ex parte Factortame Ltd (No. 2)* [1991] 1 AC 603 (HL), Lord

ACKNOWLEDGEMENTS

Bridge; Extract on page 51 from *Francovich* v *Italy Case C-9/90* [1995] ICR 722, Mischo, AG; Extract on page 61 from *Morris* v *Crown Office* [1970] 2 QB 114 (CA); Extract on page 62 from *Attorney General* v *Dallas* [2012] EWHC 156 (Admin) (AC); Extract on page 80 from *Bradlaugh* v *Gossett* (1884) 12 QBD 271 (DC); Extract on page 82 from *R* v *Graham-Campbell and others, ex parte Herbert* [1935] 1 KB 594 (DC); Extract on page 84 from *Rivlin* v *Bilainkin* [1953] 1 QB 485 (QBD); Extract on page 95 from *Malone* v *Metropolitan Police Commissioner (No. 2)* [1979] Ch 344 (CH); Extract on page 98 from *R (on the application of H)* v *London North and East Region Mental Health Review Tribunal* [2002] QB 1 (CA); Extract on page 99 from *Wilson* v *First County Trust Ltd* [2002] QB 74 (CA); Extract on page 113 from *DPP* v *Whyte* [1972] AC 849 (HL); Extract on page 113 from *Calder (John) (Publications) Ltd* v *Powell* [1965] 1 QB 509 (QB); Extract on page 116 from *Shaw* v *DPP* [1962] AC 220 (HL); Extract on page 116 from *R* v *Lemon* [1979] AC 617 (HL); Extract on page 117 from *R* v *Chief Metropolitan Stipendary Magistrate, ex parte Choudhury* [1991] 1 QB 429 (QB); Extract on page 118 from *Secretary of State for Defence* v *Guardian Newspapers Ltd* [1985] AC 339 (HL); Extract on page 122 from *Flockhart* v *Robinson* [1950] 2 KB 498 (DC); Extract on page 125 from *Chief Constable of the Bedfordshire Police* v *Golding and another* [2015] EWHC 1875 (QB); Extract on page 134 from *Rice* v *Connolly* [1966] 2 QB 414 (QB); Extract on page 141 from *Walker* v *Commissioner of Police of the Metropolis* [2015] 1 WLR 312 (CA); Extract on page 142 from *Christie* v *Leachinsky* [1947] AC 573 (HL); Extract on page 155 from R v *Inland Revenue, ex parte National Federation of Self-employed and Small Businesses* [1982] AC 617 (HL); Extract on page 156 from *Council of Civil Service Unions* v *Minister for the Civil Service (the 'GCHQ case')* [1985] AC 374 (HL); Extract on page 157 from *Attorney General* v *Fulham Corporation* [1921] 1 Ch 440 (CH); Extract on page 158 from *R* v *Richmond upon Thames London Borough Council, ex parte McCarthy & Stone (Developments) Ltd* [1992] 2 AC 48 (HL); Extract on page 159 from *Barnard* v *National Dock Labour Board* [1953] 2 QB 18 (CA); Extract on page 159 from *Associated Provincial Picture Houses Ltd* v *Wednesbury Corporation* [1948] 1 KB 223 (CA); Extract on page 160 from *R* v *Secretary of State for the Home Department, ex parte Brind* [1991] 1 AC 696 (HL); Extract on page 163 from *R* v *Bow Street Metropolitan Stipendary Magistrates' Court, ex parte Pinochet Ugarte (No. 2)* [2000] 1 AC 119 (HL); Extract on page 164 from *Porter* v *Magill* [2002] 2 AC 357 (HL); Extract on page 164 from *Ridge* v *Baldwin* [1964] AC 40 (HL); Extract on page 165 from *R* v *Secretary of State for the Home Department, ex parte Doody* [1994] 1 AC 531 (HL); Extract on page 166 from *R* v *North and East Devon Health Authority, ex p Coughlan* [2001] QB 213 (CA).

Introduction

Constitutional and Administrative Law is one of the core subjects required for a qualifying law degree and so is a compulsory part of undergraduate law programmes and graduate diploma in law programmes. It is, however, very different from many of the other core legal subjects as it concentrates less on legal rules than on the operation of the system itself, in particular, the operation of the state and the relationship between the state and the individual.

Constitutional law is often described as where law meets politics, and there are frequent references to the political process, which directly influences the law which is introduced. Much of the law we work with originates in Parliament in the form of statute, and so we must understand how Parliament works and how such statutes are produced. Similarly, in order to appreciate the role played by the common law, we must understand the position of the courts within the constitution. More importantly, constitutional law considers how power is exercised by the state and how those in power are held accountable. This includes the protection of civil liberties, and mechanisms for the individual to challenge the exercise of state power.

It is not uncommon to approach constitutional law for the first time with a certain amount of uncertainty, especially if politics is not your favourite subject, but don't worry. Almost all students find themselves enjoying the subject more than they expected and your knowledge of how 'the system' works will be invaluable in your other legal studies. The most important thing to remember is that, because we don't have a written constitution, there is no central set of rules which dictates how the state should operate. Instead, our constitutional system is a web of principles and customs which often appear outdated and vague, so don't worry if this subject seems disjointed when compared with other areas of law and don't assume that it is just you who doesn't understand – just remember the basic principles and take a little time to think about *why* the constitution has evolved into the system we have today.

Remember that this is a revision guide, not a core text, so it can never provide you with the depth of understanding which you will need to excel in examinations and it will be no substitute for structured reading around the various topics. What it can do, however, is to focus your revision on the key areas and highlight those additional points which examiners are looking for. The single most common failing in constitutional law examinations is that students write 'common sense' answers, without sufficient reference to the cases and legal principles. We all know (or think we know) what government or Parliament are, but that is not enough – as in any other area of legal writing, you need to produce logical, reasoned arguments supported by relevant authorities if you are to achieve the highest grades.

📖 **REVISION NOTE**

Throughout your revision, use the questions on the companion website to check your understanding of the subject, and to identify areas where you may want to focus your revision.

Guided tour

How to use features in the book 📖 and the companion **website** 🖱

Understand quickly

📖 **Topic maps** – Visual guides highlight key subject areas and facilitate easy navigation through the chapter. Download them from the companion website to pin on your wall or add to your revision notes.

📖 **Key definitions** – Make sure you understand essential legal terms.

📖 **Key cases and key statutes** – Identify and review the important elements of the essential cases and statutes you will need to know for your exams.

📖 **Read to impress** – These carefully selected sources will extend your knowledge, deepen your understanding, and help you to earn better marks in coursework and exams.

📖 **Glossary** – Forgotten the meaning of a word? This quick reference covers key definitions and other useful terms.

🖱 **Test your knowledge** – How well do you know each topic? Test yourself with quizzes tailored specifically to each chapter.

Revise effectively

📖 **Revision checklists** – Identify essential points you should know for your exams. The chapters will help you revise each point to ensure you are fully prepared. Print the checklists from the companion website to track your progress.

📖 **Revision notes** – These boxes highlight related points and areas where your course might adopt a particular approach that you should check with your course tutor.

🖱 **Flashcards** – Test and improve recall of important legal terms, key cases and statutes. Available in both electronic and printable formats.

Take exams with confidence

Sample questions with answer guidelines – Practice makes perfect! Consider how you would answer the question at the start of each chapter then refer to answer guidance at the end of the chapter. Try out additional sample questions online.

Assessment advice – Use this feature to identify how a subject may be examined and how to apply your knowledge effectively.

Make your answer stand out – Impress your examiners with these sources of further thinking and debate.

Exam tips – Feeling the pressure? These boxes indicate how you can improve your exam performance when it really counts.

Don't be tempted to – Spot common pitfalls and avoid losing marks.

You be the marker – Evaluate sample exam answers and understand how and why an examiner awards marks.

Table of cases and statutes

■ Cases

Agricultural, Horticultural and Forestry Industry Training Board v Aylesbury Mushrooms Ltd [1972] 1 All ER 280 (QB) **161, 203**

Anisminic Ltd v Foreign Compensation Commission [1969] 1 All ER 208 (HL) **167, 204**

Antoine v Sharma [2007] 1 WLR 780, Lord Bingham **44, 197**

Associated Provincial Picture Houses Ltd v Wednesbury Corporation [1948] 1 KB 223 (CA) **159, 203**

Attorney General v Dallas [2012] EWHC 156 (Admin) (AC) **62, 198**

Attorney General v De Keyser's Royal Hotel Ltd [1920] AC 508 (HL) **24, 25, 196, 206**

Attorney General v Fulham Corporation [1921] 1 Ch 440 (CH) **157, 202**

Attorney General v Hawkins [2013] EWHC 1455 (Admin) (DC) **62, 198**

Attorney General v Liddle [2013] EWHC 1455 (Admin) (DC) **62, 198**

Barnard v National Dock Labour Board [1953] 2 QB 18 (CA) **158, 203**

BBC v Johns (Inspector of Taxes) [1965] Ch 32 (CA) **23, 196**

Benkharbouche and another v Embassy of the Republic of Sudan (Secretary of State for Foreign and Commonwealth Affairs and others intervening) [2015] EWCA Civ 33 (CA) **100**

Bradlaugh v Gossett (1884) 12 QBD 271 (DC) **82, 198**

British Railways Board v Pickin [1974] AC 765 (HL) **48, 197**

Calder (John) (Publications) Ltd v Powell [1965] 1 QB 509 (QB) **115, 201**

Campbell v Mirror Group Newspapers (MGN) Ltd [2004] UKHL 22 (HL) **102, 200**

Chief Constable of the Bedfordshire Police v Golding and another [2015] EWHC 1875 (QB) **125, 201**

Christie v Leachinsky [1947] AC 573 (HL) **142, 202**

Collins v Wilcock [1984] 1 WLR 1172 (CA) **141**

Congreve v Home Office [1976] QB 629 (CA) **20, 196**

Council of Civil Service Unions v Minister for the Civil Service [1985] AC 374 (HL) **25, 26, 156, 165, 196, 202**

Dillon v Balfour (1887) 20 LR Ir 600 (Ct TBC) **84, 199**

Dimes v Grand Junction Canal (1852) 3 HL Cas 759 (HL) **163, 203**

Douglas v Hello Ltd [2001] 2 All ER 289 (CA) **103, 200**

DPP v Whyte [1972] AC 849 (HL) **114, 201**

Duport Steel Ltd and others v Sirs and others [1980] 1 All ER 529 (HL) **20, 196**

Entick v Carrington (1765) 19 State Tr 1029 (Ct of CP) **19, 44, 196, 197**

Flockhart v Robinson [1950] 2 KB 498 (DC) **121, 201**

Francovich v Italy Case C-9/90 [1995] ICR 722, Mischo, AG **50, 198**

GCHQ Case. See Council of Civil Service Unions v Minister for the Civil Service

Gough v United Kingdom (2014) 38 BHRC 281 (ECtHR) **113, 201**

Gouriet v Union of Post Office Workers [1978] AC 435 (HL) **25, 196**

TABLE OF CASES AND STATUTES

▉ Statutes

TABLE OF CASES AND STATUTES

The constitution
of the UK

1

Revision checklist

Essential points you should know:

☐ What is meant by the term 'constitution'?

☐ The difference between a written and an unwritten constitution

☐ The characteristics of both types of constitution

☐ The advantages and disadvantages of written and unwritten constitutions

▉ Topic map

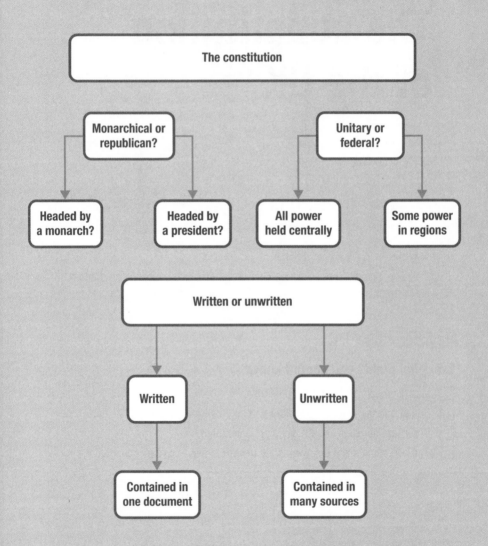

■ Introduction

What is a constitution anyway?

Before you can discuss the operation of the constitution, you need to know what we mean by the term and the answer to this is not as easy as it might first appear. The UK is different from almost every other country in the world in that we do not have a written constitution. Instead, our constitution is a web of mainly unwritten rules and this has serious implications for the way in which 'the system' works.

ASSESSMENT ADVICE

Essay questions

Essay questions on the unwritten constitution are an old favourite of examiners. Often, questions will ask you to compare and contrast our unwritten constitution with the more common written constitution (as found in countries such as the USA). Alternatively, an essay question may ask you to consider the extent to which the constitution provides protection for an individual's civil liberties in the UK. Both types of question are fairly straightforward if you appreciate the main differences between the unwritten and written systems, and it is possible to achieve high marks by making sure that you not only describe the constitution, but also offer some analysis or criticism of how it operates.

Problem questions

Problem questions on the constitution are fairly uncommon, although the way in which the unwritten constitution influences the operation of the state can be mentioned in almost any public law question. More likely is a question which may be posed as a scenario but which is, in reality, more of an essay question and simply requires you to address the same material as you would in an essay question (see example).

■ Sample question

Could you answer this question? Below is a typical essay question that could arise on this topic. Guidelines on answering the question are included at the end of this chapter, whilst a sample problem question and guidance on tackling it can be found on the companion website.

ESSAY QUESTION

'The fact that the UK does not have a written constitution is of no practical significance to the individual.' Discuss.

■ What is a constitution?

A **'constitution'** simply means a system of rules. Many organisations and clubs have constitutions which set out how people are appointed to run the club and the rules which affect the club's members. In the same way, the constitution of a country sets out how power is held by the state and how that power relates to the citizen. In this way, the constitution can be said to define both a *horizontal* relationship (between the various institutions of state) and a *vertical* relationship (between the state and the individual).

KEY DEFINITION: Constitution

The framework of rules which dictate the way in which power is divided between the various parts of the state and the relationship between the state and the individual.

Figure 1.1

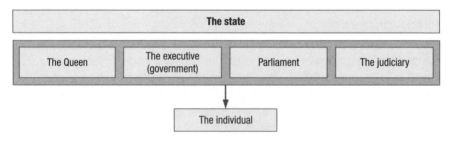

In most other countries, this system of rules is contained in a single document which is called 'the constitution', and this illustrates that there are two ways in which the term 'constitution' can be interpreted: first, as a system of rules; and, second, as a piece of paper which sets out that system of rules. This is an important distinction when comparing the unwritten constitution of the UK with other countries (such as the USA) which have a written constitution.

■ Types of constitution

Before considering the differences between the unwritten constitution of the UK and the written constitutions of most other countries, it is also possible to identify other ways in which constitutions can be classified:

Monarchical and republican constitutions

Under a **'monarchical' constitution**, the head of state is a king or queen and state powers are exercised in their name. In this way, although the majority of power in the UK now resides with Parliament and the government, the Queen remains the head of state.

By contrast, a **'republican' constitution** has as its head of state a president, who has far more power than the current Queen. Such powers are justified on the basis that the president is elected and so accountable to the people, unlike a monarch, who is head of state simply by birth.

KEY DEFINITION: Monarchical and republican constitution

A monarchical constitution is based on the historical power of a monarch who acts as head of state and in whose name power is exercised by the government.

A republican constitution has an elected president as the head of state, who exercises power in the name of the state.

Federal and unitary constitutions

In some countries, state powers are divided into those exercised by central government and those exercised by the states or regions. This results in a **'federal' constitution**.

For example, in the USA, central government (also known as the 'federal' government) retains the most important powers relating to matters such as defence, whereas the individual 'states' have powers on a local level and have their own constitutional status.

By contrast, the UK has a **'unitary' constitution** where all power resides in the central state institutions. We do have local government, in the form of local councils, but these can be altered (or even abolished) by the central government at any time.

KEY DEFINITION: Federal and unitary constitution

A federal constitution has a division of powers between the central government and the governments of individual states or regions.

A unitary constitution has power concentrated in central government. Local government may exist but not with the constitutional status of the states under a federal constitution.

 Make your answer stand out

Examiners will expect to see a discussion of the differences between written and unwritten constitutions. It is less common for students to mention the other ways in which constitutions may be categorised, and so mentioning these will make your answer stand out from the crowd. You could include the example of the abolition of the Greater London Council by the government in 1985 as an example of the power remaining with central government under a unitary constitution (the federal government of the USA could not abolish one of the states in this way under the federal system), and you could also discuss whether it is preferable to have an elected president, under a republican constitution, or an unelected monarch, as in the UK.

■ Written and unwritten constitutions

The most important way to classify constitutions is between 'written' and 'unwritten'.

Written constitutions

As has already been mentioned, almost every country apart from the UK has a written constitution which contains the main rules governing the power of the state and the relationship between the state and the individual in a single document. For the citizens of the country, the constitution is an enormously important document because it prevents the state from abusing its powers and safeguards the rights of the individual.

Changing a written constitution

In order to protect the citizen against the state, the constitution has to be strong (otherwise the government will simply change it), but if it is too strong, then it cannot be amended to reflect changes in society. For example, the original US constitution included the right to own slaves, which was later removed when the majority recognised this as unacceptable. This requires a delicate balance between a constitution which is rigid and entrenched and one which is sufficiently flexible to reflect changes in society.

Key provisions of the Constitution of the United States of America

Article 1: establishes the first branch of government – the legislature.

Article 2: establishes the second branch of government – the executive.

Article 3: establishes the third branch of government – the judiciary.

Article 4: provides that all states must honour the laws of the other states.

Article 5: outlines the procedure for amending the constitution.

✎ EXAM TIP

Make sure to point out that many written constitutions are produced after a revolution, where the citizens rise up against what they see as an oppressive state. In this way the US constitution was written after the War of Independence from Britain, and the French constitution was produced after the French Revolution. You can also make the point that, although most countries have a written constitution, the UK is not the only country without such a document. Both New Zealand and Israel also have unwritten constitutions.

Unwritten constitutions

By contrast, countries such as the UK with an unwritten constitution have no single document which sets out power relationships within the state. Instead, we have many sources, both written and unwritten, which combine to provide the rules regulating the state. These sources are discussed in the next chapter.

📖 REVISION NOTE

The unwritten constitution of the UK can be brought into every topic within constitutional and administrative law. For example, examiners will frequently set questions on specific sources of the constitution, such as **royal prerogative** or **constitutional conventions**, but always remember to discuss these in the context of the unwritten constitution and emphasise that you understand that such sources are important because they operate as part of the unwritten system. Examiners will give you credit for making such connections between different parts of the syllabus.

Rights and the constitution

One of the most important aspects of a written constitution is that it provides protection for individual rights. For example, the US constitution specifically lists a number of rights as amendments to the constitution (e.g. the First Amendment – the right to freedom of speech). Such rights cannot be taken away by the state. Under an unwritten constitution, the state can take away individual rights at any time because they are not protected by the constitution.

 Make your answer stand out

As an example of the protection of rights under a written constitution and the vulnerability of rights under the unwritten system of the UK, cite the ease with which the government was able to drastically reduce gun ownership in the UK by means of the Firearms (Amendment) Act 1997 following the Dunblane massacre of the previous year. By contrast, the right to bear arms is enshrined in the US constitution and, as a consequence, has proved almost impossible to restrict.

✎ EXAM TIP

In considering the status of individual rights in the UK, remember that, although the unwritten constitution does not protect rights, we now have the European Convention on Human Rights, as implemented by the Human Rights Act 1998, which does provide greater protection for certain rights. Impress the examiner by making a brief comparison between the protection afforded to individual rights under the European Convention and the more entrenched protection provided by a written constitution.

■ Characteristics of written and unwritten constitutions

Almost all exam questions on the unwritten constitution will ask you to outline the key characteristics of both written and unwritten constitutions and to compare their strengths and weaknesses. This type of comparison demonstrates the analytical skills which examiners want to see in answers.

Written constitutions

Advantages	Disadvantages
All key provisions are contained in a single document.	Requires one document to encompass the regulation of the entire constitution.
Provides a clear statement of how the state should operate with no uncertainty over words. Everyone can read and agree what it says.	May lead to litigation over the precise meanings of the terms used, particularly if the language is outdated.
Protects the individual from abuses by the government of the day.	May be difficult to amend if the provisions become outdated (e.g. the USA and slavery).
Provides clear protection of individual rights.	May be inflexible and unresponsive to change.

Unwritten constitutions

Advantages	Disadvantages
Flexible and responsive to changing circumstances.	Can appear vague and uncertain. No single agreed source of constitutional law.
Leaves the state free to develop the law for the benefit of citizens.	Leaves the state free to abuse its powers and develop laws which act against its citizens.
Encourages the evolution of the constitution.	Provides no protection for individual civil liberties.

■ Could the UK ever have a written constitution?

Demands for a written constitution in the UK are not new and regularly appear in the press and in Parliament. It should be recognised, however, that producing such a document would be an enormous task which would be sure to encounter fierce opposition from those who value the unique flexibility of the existing system. In addition, a public debate on the wording of a possible constitution would draw attention to the relationship between the UK and Europe, which none of the main parties is likely to welcome.

■ Putting it all together

Answer guidelines

See the essay question at the start of the chapter.

Approaching the question

- Adopt a clear structure which approaches each part of the answer in turn.
- First make clear what is meant by the word 'constitution', then address the various characteristics which a constitution may have.
- Remember that the focus is on the differences between a written and unwritten constitution.
- Make full use of your conclusion to offer some genuine reflection and analysis on the question posed by the examiner.

Important points to include

- Recognise the two key relationships which are defined by the constitution: between the organs of the state and between the state and the individual.
- Set out the key characteristics of the UK constitution as monarchical (rather than republican) and unitary (rather than federal).
- Work through the advantages and disadvantages of written and unwritten constitutions listed above.
- It could be argued that our constitution appears to work reasonably well because we are a prosperous society with relative freedom.
- But you can also consider the negligible protection for individual rights provided by the UK constitution. Because the state is not constrained by a written constitution, it can change the law and remove our rights.
- You could conclude that the constitution of the UK has worked well, but that if something does go wrong, there is little protection for the individual to be found in the constitution.
- Also, show that you are aware of recent developments by referring to the 2012 report of the Commission on a Bill of Rights (discussed further in Chapter 6).

Make your answer stand out

- Remember to read the question carefully. Is it asking you to list the characteristics of the constitution or (as in this question) assess the impact on the individual citizen?

- Do not simply divide constitutions between written and unwritten but also consider the other ways in which constitutions can be defined (federal/unitary; monarchical/republican). Most students only mention written/unwritten, so this additional discussion will earn extra credit.

- Note that the question does not simply require description (what the constitution is) but also analysis (how well it works). Students always do well on description but fall down on analysis. For this reason, the best way to increase your overall mark is to demonstrate that you can weigh up the advantages and disadvantages.

- Always draw your arguments together into a proper conclusion which expresses a view on the central question and which is based on the points you have raised in your answer.

READ TO IMPRESS

Beatson, J. (2010) Reforming an unwritten constitution. *Law Quarterly Review*, 126: 48–71.

Bindman, G. (2013) Deadlock and a fudge. *New Law Journal*, 163: 8.

Blackburn, R. (2015) Enacting a written constitution for the United Kingdom. *Statute Law Review*, 36(1): 1.

Bogdanor, V. (ed.) (2003) *The British Constitution in the Twentieth Century*. Oxford: Oxford University Press.

Bogdanor, V. (2004) Our new constitution. *Law Quarterly Review*, 120: 242–62.

Elliott, M. (2007) Bicameralism, sovereignty and the unwritten constitution. *International Journal of Constitutional Law*, 5: 370–79.

Galligan, D. J. (2008) The paradox of constitutionalism or the potential of constitutional theory? *Oxford Journal of Legal Studies*, 28: 343–67.

Goldsworthy, J. (2003) Homogenising constitutions. *Oxford Journal of Legal Studies*, 23: 483. ▶

Juss, S. S. (2006) Constitutionalising rights without a constitution: the British experience under Article 6 of the Human Rights Act 1998. *Statute Law Review*, 27: 1–32.

Kay, R. S. (1989) Substance and structure as constitutional protections: centennial comparisons. *Public Law*, 428–39.

Laws, J. (2012) The good constitution. *The Cambridge Law Journal*, 71: 567–82.

Sedley, S. (1994) The sound of silence: constitutional law without a constitution. *Law Quarterly Review*, 110: 270–91.

Singh, R. (2008) Interpreting bills of rights. *Statute Law Review*, 29: 82–99.

Walker, N. (2000) Beyond the unitary conception of the United Kingdom constitution. *Public Law*, 384–404.

www.pearsoned.co.uk/lawexpress

 Go online to access more revision support including quizzes to test your knowledge, sample questions with answer guidelines, printable versions of the topic maps, and more!

Where does the constitution come from?

2

■ Topic map

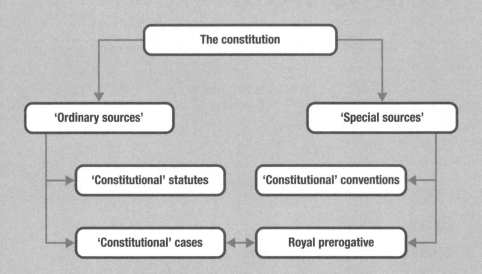

■ Introduction

The state operates in accordance with rules but, to apply the rules, it is first necessary to understand where they come from.

One of the problems with an unwritten constitution is that there is no single document which sets out how the state works and where the power lies. Instead, this information comes from a number of different sources. This area is relatively straightforward but, in answering exam questions, it is important to show that you understand the differences between the various sources and also how they work together. Examiners usually concentrate on the 'special' sources when setting questions, but be aware that you may find references to constitutional sources in questions on other topics, such as parliamentary sovereignty or separation of powers.

ASSESSMENT ADVICE

Essay questions

Essay questions on the sources of constitutional law provide an excellent opportunity for the well-prepared student to demonstrate their knowledge, and here the most important point to remember is the distinction between the 'ordinary' and 'special' sources and the ways in which constitutional conventions and royal prerogative are very different from statute and common law. It is more common, however, for examiners to concentrate on the 'special' sources and to set a more detailed question on the operation of either constitutional conventions or royal prerogative. Here, the examiner will be looking for both a clear statement of the characteristics of the source and, in particular, its status as 'non-legal' rules. Also, remember that the better answer will always include a number of examples.

Problem questions

Problem questions on constitutional sources are not common, as the subject lends itself much more to essays, but it is possible that an imaginative examiner may seek to test students with a series of scenarios, each illustrating one of the sources. More likely is a problem which concentrates on either constitutional conventions or royal prerogative and here the key point which the examiner will want you to address will be the difficulties in enforcing such rules through the courts. Once again, the use of examples is crucial to achieving a high mark.

Sample question

Could you answer this question? Below is a typical essay question that could arise on this topic. Guidelines on answering the question are included at the end of this chapter, whilst a sample problem question and guidance on tackling it can be found on the companion website.

ESSAY QUESTION

The constitution of England and Wales is to be found not in a single document, but in a range of sources. Discuss.

Sources of the constitution

One of the key differences between the UK and a country with a written constitution is that we cannot look to a single document to explain how the state operates. Instead, we must consider a variety of sources which provide the rules governing how the state should operate. It is important to realise that, because there is no central 'blueprint' for how the state works (in the form of a written constitution), there is nothing to prevent these various rules from coming into conflict, and this does occur. As a result, this can be a confusing area to study. However, it is not as difficult as it may first appear, providing that you approach the various sources in turn, taking some time to understand the differences between them. You should also take some time before the examination to make sure that you not only know the differences but can articulate them on paper.

Ordinary sources

In considering the sources of the constitution, it is possible to make a distinction between what are sometimes termed 'ordinary' and 'special' sources. This simply means that some constitutional sources are viewed as 'ordinary' because they also apply in other areas of law, such as contract, tort, etc., whereas the 'special' sources are to be found only in the study of constitutional and administrative law. Because the ordinary sources are more familiar, it is advisable to begin with those.

Statute

Perhaps the most familiar source of law is statute and, as with every other area of law, there are many Acts of Parliament which impact on the operation of the constitution. Such Acts may set out specific powers of the state or, alternatively, provide protections for the citizen.

✎ EXAM TIP

Although the constitution of the UK is described as 'unwritten', this just means that it is not contained within a single document. The existence of statutes which are 'constitutional' in their effect means that there are a large number of sources of constitutional law which are, indeed, written. For this reason, rather than simply stating that 'the UK has an unwritten constitution', point out that there are written sources which impact upon the operation of the constitution, but that what is lacking is a *single* document setting out the powers of the state. Also, emphasise that, over time, many of the 'special' sources have been replaced by statutory powers in order to make them more accountable to Parliament and the courts.

Identifying a 'constitutional' statute

Although many statutes have a constitutional significance, they are not always easy to identify. This is because, unlike other areas of law, the title of the Act does not provide a clear indication of its relevance. For example, whereas it is clear that the Unfair Contract Terms Act 1977 has something to do with the law of contract and that the Theft Act 1968 relates to the criminal offence of theft, it is rare for an Act of Parliament to contain a reference to the constitution in its title. For this reason, we must look elsewhere in order to identify a 'constitutional' statute.

KEY CASE

Thoburn v *Sunderland City Council* [2002] EWHC 195 (Admin)

Concerning: defining 'constitutional' sources

Facts

A number of market traders were prosecuted for selling fruit and vegetables by the pound, rather than by the kilogram as required by the Metrication Directive (Council Directive (EEC) 80/181)). The defendants appealed against conviction, challenging the authority of the amendments which had been made to the Weights and Measures Act 1985.

Legal principle

In dismissing the appeals, the court clarified the distinction between 'ordinary' and 'constitutional' statutes. Laws LJ: 'In my opinion a constitutional statute is one which (a) conditions the legal relationship between citizen and State in some general, overarching manner, or (b) enlarges or diminishes the scope of what we would now regard as fundamental constitutional rights'.

Make your answer stand out

Another key feature of a 'constitutional' statute is that it is not subject to the doctrine of implied repeal. As Laws LJ made clear in Thoburn, 'Ordinary statutes may be impliedly repealed. Constitutional statutes may not.'

Therefore, the key to deciding which statutes are 'constitutional' is to ask: 'Does the Act impact on either the workings of the state or on the relationship between the state and the individual?' In this way, we look not at the name of the statute but to its effects.

Some 'constitutional' statutes

KEY STATUTE

Act of Union with Scotland 1707

United England and Scotland, giving power to the Westminster Parliament to legislate over Scotland.

Bill of Rights 1689

Established Parliament (rather than the monarch) as the supreme law-making body in England. Restricted the powers of the king and set out basic individual rights.

Parliament Acts 1911 and 1949

Removed the ability of the House of Lords to reject legislation which has been passed by the House of Commons, leaving only the power to delay Bills for a fixed period of time.

His Majesty's Declaration of Abdication Act 1936

Allowed King Edward VIII to give up the throne in order to marry US divorcee Wallis Simpson.

Human Rights Act 1998

Made domestic courts 'courts of human rights' by providing direct access to many of the rights contained in the European Convention on Human Rights. Placed a statutory obligation on the state to act in accordance with the Convention rights.

House of Lords Act 1999

Removed the rights of the majority of hereditary peers to sit and vote in the House of Lords.

Constitutional Reform Act 2005

Modified the role of the Lord Chancellor and established the Supreme Court.

Fixed-term Parliaments Act 2011

Introduced a set date for the next general election (removing from the Prime Minister the discretion to select the election date).

European Union (Notification of Withdrawal) Act 2017

Authorised the government to trigger Article 50, beginning the process of withdrawal from the EU.

Common law

The second of our 'ordinary sources' of constitutional law is the common law and there are many judicial decisions which impact on the working of the constitution. As with statute, the difficulty is in establishing precisely which cases have this effect and, once again, the best way of approaching any discussion is by reference to example. You should always include a number of such authorities to support your arguments.

📖 **REVISION NOTE**

When discussing the role of the common law within the constitution, point out that there are constitutional issues where the courts seek to restrict the powers of the state. Such conflicts highlight the constitutional importance of an independent judiciary as part of the 'separation of powers' (see Chapter 4).

KEY CASE

Entick v *Carrington* (1765) 19 State Tr 1029 (Ct of CP)

Concerning: the limits of state powers

Facts

The king's messengers broke into Entick's house on orders from the Secretary of State to seize both Entick and his papers (he was suspected of treason). Entick challenged the legality of the search but the Secretary of State argued that such powers were an essential part of government.

Legal principle

The state had to act within legal authority. Therefore, if there was no statute or common law precedent which authorised the search, it would be illegal. The state was not above the law. Lord Camden CJ: 'If this was law it would be found in our books, but no such law ever existed in this country.'

KEY CASE

Duport Steel Ltd and others v *Sirs and others* [1980] 1 All ER 529 (HL)

Concerning: the relationship between Parliament and the courts

Facts

A union called a strike of its members. The court was required to decide whether the union's actions were 'in furtherance of a trade dispute', as required by the relevant Act of Parliament.

Legal principle

Sets out the relationship between Parliament and the courts. Lord Diplock: 'Parliament makes the laws, the judiciary interpret them'.

KEY CASE

Congreve v *Home Office* [1976] QB 629 (CA)

Concerning: the powers of the executive

Facts

The government decided to raise the cost of a TV licence, but, after the planned increase was announced, a number of people bought new licences at the old price before the increase came into effect. In order to recover the money lost, the government decided to revoke the licences unless the increased fee was paid.

Legal principle

The actions proposed by the government amounted to a tax which had not been authorised by Parliament. The government could only levy taxes on the public where Parliament had expressly authorised them to do so. Lane LJ: '[This is] a means of extracting money which Parliament has given the executive no mandate to demand.'

□ REVISION NOTE

Discussion of the common law as a source of constitutional law raises issues of parliamentary sovereignty and the separation of powers (Chapter 3). In looking at both of these topics, you will see that, although the courts must follow the will of Parliament, they are able to challenge wrongdoing on the part of the executive.

Make your answer stand out

In discussing 'constitutional' cases, make sure to mention *R (on the application of Miller)* v *Secretary of State for Exiting the European Union* [2017] UKSC 5 (SC), which concerned the power of the government to trigger the Article 50 Brexit process. See Chapter 11 for details.

As you can see, statute and common law act as sources of constitutional law, much as they do in other areas of law. For this reason, the key to a good answer is to include examples, such as those above, to illustrate the ways in which Parliament and the courts have shaped the rules of the constitution. You should also emphasise the clarity and certainty of statute and common law when compared with the 'special' sources.

■ Special sources

Having considered the 'ordinary' sources of statute and common law, we must now examine those sources of law which are particular to constitutional and administrative law. Unlike their more familiar counterparts, these sources do not appear in other legal subjects and so they can, initially, appear confusing. The key to understanding how they operate is to recognise that their origins lie not in Parliament, but in the history of England.

Royal prerogative

There remain a number of important powers within the constitution which fall under the title '**royal prerogative**' or 'prerogative powers' and which have their origins in the powers originally exercised by the monarch. Although Parliament is now the most powerful of the institutions of state, the **executive** can still exercise a number of powers without the consent of either Parliament or the courts, and this absence of accountability makes such powers particularly useful to government.

KEY DEFINITION: Royal prerogative

This was defined by Dicey as 'the residue of discretionary or arbitrary authority . . . legally left in the Hands of the Crown . . . the remaining portion of the Crown's original authority' (see Dicey (1885)).

It is possible to divide such powers into those relating to foreign affairs and those relating to domestic affairs. It is also possible to make a distinction between those powers which are exercised by the monarch and those which are exercised by the government.

❗ Don't be tempted to . . .

Meaning of 'the Crown'

Be clear on the use of the term 'the Crown'. This does not just mean the Queen but also means the government, which acts 'in the name of the Crown'.

Example

'Foreign' prerogatives

Declarations of war and peace

The Crown can declare war without the permission of Parliament.

Making treaties

The Crown has authority to make treaties with foreign countries.

The issue of passports

The Crown controls the issue of passports.

Example

'Domestic' prerogatives

Appointment of the Prime Minister

The monarch appoints the Prime Minister.

Dissolution of Parliament

The monarch retains the power to summon and to dissolve Parliament.

Royal assent

The monarch has the power to give royal assent to an Act of Parliament and must do so before it can come into force.

Who exercises the power?

It is also possible to make a distinction between powers which are exercised by the monarch personally and those which are exercised by the government in the name of the Crown. In this way, the Queen retains the power to appoint the Prime Minister and to prorogue and dissolve Parliament, whereas the government exercises prerogative powers such as the making of international treaties and the granting of passports. There are also powers, such as the appointment of ministers, which are exercised by the Queen but on the advice of the Prime Minister. Although the use of the term 'advice' suggests that the Queen could ignore the wishes of the Prime Minister if she wished, in practical terms she is bound to appoint those chosen by the elected leader.

 Make your answer stand out

The continuing existence of prerogative powers is the cause of some concern for those who would prefer to see all state power accountable to Parliament. There have been attempts to table legislation to bring such powers under the control of Parliament, but the government inevitably fails to support such measures – preferring to retain the powers without interference from Parliament. One important example which can be used to enhance your answer is the discussion surrounding the use of prerogative power by the government to agree an extradition treaty with the USA without the approval of Parliament. Many view the treaty as 'one-sided', giving far greater powers to the USA than to the UK. For discussion of the issues, see: Smith (2005); Harrington (2006); Poole (2010). For a more recent discussion of the status of such prerogative powers, see also *R (on the application of Barclay and another) v Secretary of State for Justice and Lord Chancellor and others* [2014] UKSC 54.

Because prerogative powers are a residue of the original powers of the monarch, it is not possible to create new prerogative powers.

KEY CASE

BBC v Johns (Inspector of Taxes) [1965] Ch 32 (CA)

Concerning: the possibility of creating new prerogative powers

Facts

The BBC attempted to argue that, because it had been established by Royal Charter, it was part of 'the Crown' and so exempt from paying tax.

Legal principle

It was held that the BBC could not escape paying taxes in this way. The historical exemption from taxation which applied to the Crown could not be extended to the Corporation. In a famous comment, Lord Diplock: 'it is 350 years and a civil war too late for the Queen's court to broaden the prerogative'.

However, there would seem to be a fine line between creating a new prerogative and merely reinterpreting an old one.

KEY CASE

Malone v Metropolitan Police Commissioner (No. 2) **[1979] Ch 344 (CH)**
Concerning: the widening of prerogative

Facts

The plaintiff, an antiques dealer, was tried on charges of receiving stolen goods. During the trial it was revealed that his telephone had been tapped on the basis of a warrant issued by the Secretary of State. The plaintiff asserted that the Crown had no power, under either statute or common law, to tap telephones.

Legal principle

It was held that, because there was no express law against telephone tapping, the Secretary of State's actions were lawful. There was also an acknowledgement that, because there had existed a historical prerogative power to intercept letters, there must also be a power to intercept telephone calls. Megarry VC: 'it can lawfully be done simply because there is nothing to make it unlawful'.

Prerogative powers and statute

It is established that, where a prerogative power and a statutory power come into conflict, the statutory power will prevail. This is another expression of the doctrine of **parliamentary sovereignty**.

KEY CASE

Attorney General v De Keyser's Royal Hotel Ltd **[1920] AC 508 (HL)**
Concerning: conflict between statutory and prerogative power

Facts

During the First World War, the hotel had been used by British troops. After the war, the owners sought compensation from the British government for damage caused to the building. A statutory power, under the Defence of the Realm Act 1914, provided for compensation payments, but the government argued that their actions did not fall under the Act but instead fell under the prerogative power of defence and so no compensation was payable.

Legal principle

It was held that, where a statute is passed, it replaces the prerogative power. Parmoor L: 'It would be an untenable proposition to suggest that Courts of Law could disregard the protective restrictions imposed by statute law where they are applicable. In this respect the sovereignty of Parliament is supreme.'

✎ EXAM TIP

Although *Attorney General* v *De Keyser's Royal Hotel* established that a statutory power will take priority over a prerogative power, it seems that the prerogative power does not disappear completely but is 'kept in abeyance' while the statute is in force and can return if the statute is repealed. This is the kind of point which can greatly enhance your answers on this topic.

Prerogative powers and the courts

One of the most important aspects of prerogative powers is that, traditionally, they have not been enforceable by the courts. They have been seen as 'non-justiciable', which means that the court will recognise that a prerogative power applies in a given situation, but cannot enforce it. This made such powers largely unaccountable.

KEY CASE

Gouriet v *Union of Post Office Workers* [1978] AC 435 (HL)

Concerning: the courts and prerogative power

Facts

The union planned a strike in support of the anti-apartheid movement in South Africa. The Attorney General decided not to pursue legal action to prevent the strike. This led to accusations that he had misused his powers in order to protect the union.

Legal principle

It was held that this was a prerogative power which was vested in the Attorney General. Consequently, it was not open to the court to question how, or whether, the power was used. Viscount Dilhorne: 'In the exercise of these powers he is not subject to direction by his ministerial colleagues or to control and supervision by the courts.'

However, this position began to change with the recognition by the courts that prerogative powers were not beyond their jurisdiction.

KEY CASE

Council of Civil Service Unions v *Minister for the Civil Service (the GCHQ case)*
[1985] AC 374 (HL)

Concerning: the courts and prerogative power

Facts

It was decided by the government that workers at the secret Government Communications Headquarters (GCHQ) should not be allowed to join a trade union in case this led to them going on strike. The government altered the terms of employment of the workers, by means of prerogative power, to prohibit union membership. The union sought judicial review of the policy.

Legal principle

It was held that, although this particular prerogative power remained non-justiciable, there was nothing in principle to prevent the courts from considering the use of prerogative powers. Lord Roskill: 'I am unable to see . . . that there is any logical reason why the fact that the source of the power is the prerogative and not statute should today deprive the citizen of that right of challenge.' This has led to various prerogative powers being challenged in later cases.

! Don't be tempted to . . .

The significance of the GCHQ case

Don't underestimate the significance of the 'GCHQ case'. It is extremely important because, even though the union lost their challenge to the policy, the court recognised that it had the power to review at least some of the prerogative powers exercised by the Crown – this had previously been thought impossible.

Following the decision of the House of Lords in the GCHQ case, the courts have considered a number of prerogative powers. Some have been held to be open to judicial review but others remain non-justiciable.

KEY CASE

R v *Secretary of State for the Home Department, ex parte Northumbria Police Authority* **[1989] QB 26 (CA)**

Concerning: the courts and prerogative power

Facts

The Secretary of State indicated that he would make riot control equipment available to police forces even against the wishes of the relevant police authority. Northumbria

Police Authority challenged the policy, arguing that the Secretary of State has no power to supply such equipment to police forces against the wishes of the police authority.

Legal principle

It was held that the consent of the police authority was not required under the relevant provisions of the Police Act 1964 and, further, that the Secretary of State retained a prerogative power 'to protect the peace of the realm' which remained unaffected by the passage of the 1964 Act. Purchas LJ: 'the prerogative powers to take all reasonable steps to preserve the Queen's peace remains unaffected by the Act'.

✎ EXAM TIP

It is worth pointing out that the court appeared to take for granted the existence of a prerogative power to keep the peace, largely as a 'sister' prerogative power to that which permits the declaration of war.

KEY CASE

R v Secretary of State for Foreign and Commonwealth Affairs, ex parte Everett [1989] QB 811 (CA)

Concerning: the courts and prerogative power

Facts

The Secretary of State refused to issue a new passport to a British citizen living in Spain on the basis that he was subject to an arrest warrant in the UK. The applicant sought judicial review of the decision.

Legal principle

It was held that the prerogative power to issue passports was subject to judicial review as it was a power which affected the rights of the individual and did not have foreign policy implications. Provided that the Secretary of State communicated the reason for the refusal, together with the details of the warrant, the refusal to issue a new passport was within his powers. O'Connor LJ: 'the Secretary of State, in the fair exercise of discretion, was entitled to refuse the passport'.

KEY CASE

R v *Secretary of State for the Home Department, ex parte Bentley* [1994] QB 349
Concerning: the courts and prerogative power

Facts

The case concerned the refusal of the Secretary of State to exercise the prerogative of mercy to grant a posthumous pardon to Derek Bentley, who had been executed for the murder of a policeman in 1953. The circumstances of the original conviction had led to repeated calls for a pardon.

Legal principle

It was held that the court could review the prerogative of mercy in order to conclude that the original decision not to grant a pardon was flawed. The court would not order a pardon but would invite the Secretary of State to reconsider the decision. Watkins LJ: 'the court, though it has no power to direct the way in which the prerogative of mercy should be exercised, has some role to play'.

KEY CASE

R v *Secretary of State for Foreign and Commonwealth Affairs, ex parte Rees-Mogg* [1994] QB 552, Lloyd LJ
Concerning: the courts and prerogative power

Facts

The Prime Minister agreed the Maastricht Treaty with other European leaders, but it could not become part of UK law until ratified by Parliament. Faced with opposition from within his own party, the Prime Minister threatened to ratify the treaty without a vote, by means of prerogative power.

Legal principle

The application for judicial review would be refused. The power to ratify the treaty remained within the prerogative power of the Crown. Lloyd LJ: 'the treaty-making power is part of the royal prerogative'.

EXAM TIP

It is worth pointing out that, although the Prime Minister threatened to use prerogative power to ratify the treaty, this proved unnecessary as his MPs, fearful of losing a vote of confidence, ultimately backed him and passed the vote in Parliament.

Constitutional conventions

The other 'special source' is the constitutional convention. These are customs or historical practices which determine what will happen in certain circumstances. As with royal prerogative, conventions are not enforceable by the courts and so are described as 'non-legal' rules.

! Don't be tempted to . . .

Conventions and prerogative powers

There is a considerable overlap between the operation of constitutional conventions and royal prerogative and this can cause confusion. The best way to view the relationship between the two is that certain actions are authorised by prerogative power and the convention provides the custom or rule which dictates how the power shall be exercised. If you confuse these two areas in the examination, it is a clear indication that you do not really understand the topic – not the message that you want to send the examiner!

Example

Constitutional Conventions

Royal assent

The monarch gives royal assent by means of prerogative power – the convention is that the monarch will always give assent to a Bill which has been approved by Parliament.

Appointment of the Prime Minister

The monarch appoints the Prime Minister – by convention this is the leader of the political party with the largest number of seats in the House of Commons.

Vote of confidence

By convention, the government will resign if it loses a vote of confidence in the Commons.

There is nothing in law to enforce a convention, and it is said that the sanction is 'political' rather than 'legal'. Conventions can also change over time.

Make your answer stand out

The changing nature of conventions is particularly evident in relation to ministerial responsibility. The convention that ministers would resign if there were serious failings in their department has all but disappeared and this can be viewed in terms of a weakening of the 'political' sanction. For a discussion of recent development of constitutional conventions, see Wilson (2004).

 Make your answer stand out

Cite the recent case of *R (on the application of Evans) and another* v *Attorney General* [2015] UKSC 21 which concerned letters written by Prince Charles to ministers and which raised the 'tripartite convention', namely the ability of the sovereign to exercise her right to consult, to encourage and to warn her government and the 'education convention' that the heir to the throne should be instructed in the business of government in preparation for when he is king.

■ Putting it all together

Answer guidelines

See the essay question at the start of the chapter.

Approaching the question

- Adopt a clear and methodical structure to address the various aspects of the question in turn.
- Always support your points with examples and authorities where possible. Many students do not include cases, etc., and this is always penalised.

Important points to include

- Use a clear introduction to make, briefly, the distinction between a written and an unwritten constitution. Emphasise the absence of a central document in the UK constitution and the overlapping nature of the various sources of constitutional law.

- Address the various sources in turn, making the distinction between 'ordinary' and 'special' sources. Begin with statute and common law, which apply to this area in the same way as they apply to other areas of law. Therefore, you need to utilise examples to illustrate relevance.

- In considering the 'special' sources, acknowledge the degree of overlap between prerogative powers and constitutional conventions. Use the examples above to demonstrate how such unwritten powers operate within the constitution.

- Draw your answer together with a sizeable conclusion (not just a couple of lines) which reflects on the characteristics of the various sources. As statute and common law are well known, your answer should concentrate on prerogative powers and conventions.

 Make your answer stand out

- Always use examples to support your arguments.
- Indicate that you are aware of the impact of other aspects of the constitution on the question (such as the separation of powers and the doctrine of parliamentary sovereignty). You need not examine these in detail, but it will greatly enhance your answer to have acknowledged their relevance to the debate.
- Emphasise the essentially uncertain nature of the UK constitution and, perhaps, draw some brief comparison with countries which have a written constitution. Even a modest attempt at comparison will impress the examiner, but do not digress too much – make the point and then move on.

READ TO IMPRESS

Blackburn, R. (2004) Monarchy and the personal prerogatives. *Public Law,* 546–63.

Cohn, M. (2005) Medieval chains, invisible inks: on non-statutory powers of the executive. *Oxford Journal of Legal Studies,* 25: 97–122.

Dicey, A.V. (1885) *An Introduction to the Study of the Constitution,* 10th edn (1959). London: Macmillan.

Harrington, J. (2006) Scrutiny and approval: the role for Westminster style parliaments in treaty making. *International and Comparative Law Quarterly,* 55: 121–60.

Pontin, B. and Billings, P. (2001) Prerogative orders and the Human Rights Act: elevating the status of Orders in Council. *Public Law,* 21–27.

▶

Poole, T. (2010) United Kingdom: the royal prerogative. *International Journal of Constitutional Law,* 8(1): 146–55.

Smith, R. (2005) Right and wrongs: going over there. *Law Society Gazette,* 102.24: 18.

Squires, D.B. (2000) Judicial review of the prerogative after the Human Rights Act. *Law Quarterly Review,* 116: 572–75.

Wilson, Lord (2004) The robustness of conventions in a time of modernisation and change. *Public Law,* 407–20.

www.pearsoned.co.uk/lawexpress

Go online to access more revision support including quizzes to test your knowledge, sample questions with answer guidelines, printable versions of the topic maps, and more!

Basic principles of the constitution

3

Revision checklist

Essential points you should know:

- [ ] The constitutional importance of the principles of democracy and accountability
- [ ] The three constitutional doctrines which underpin the operation of the constitution: parliamentary sovereignty; the separation of powers; and the rule of law
- [ ] The separation of powers as a mechanism for preventing the over-concentration of power and the danger that power will be abused as a consequence
- [ ] The rule of law as a means of ensuring that all are treated fairly and that no one is above the law
- [ ] The traditional approach towards parliamentary sovereignty, which holds that Parliament is the most powerful organ of state, and the extent to which this principle has been undermined by our membership of the European Union

■ Topic map

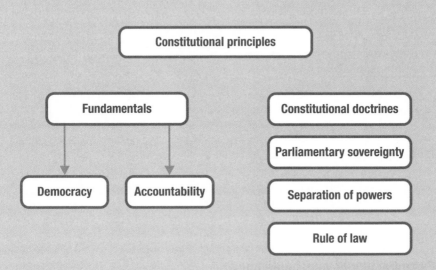

■ Introduction

The constitution may be unwritten but it operates in accordance with a number of fundamental principles.

We saw in Chapter 2 that the unwritten constitution has a number of sources, but there are also broader principles which dictate how 'the system' operates. Some of these can be described as 'constitutional doctrines', and they provide fundamental rules which dictate how the constitution works. These doctrines are common examination topics and so need to be understood. They can also be discussed in answers on other aspects of the constitution.

ASSESSMENT ADVICE

Essay questions

Essay questions on the constitutional doctrines are common and, in answering such questions, examiners will expect you not only to state what the doctrines are but also to provide some analysis, typically couched in terms of 'how important are the doctrines to the operation of the constitution' or 'to what extent have the doctrines changed'. This second type of question is particularly common in relation to parliamentary sovereignty, which has been dramatically undermined by our membership of the EU, and most examiners will want to see some understanding of how this has changed the operation of parliamentary sovereignty.

Problem questions

Problem questions on the rule of law and the separation of powers are relatively uncommon, as both lend themselves more readily to essay questions. However, examiners may choose to set a problem question on parliamentary sovereignty. As with essay questions, such problem questions will require you to outline the key aspects of parliamentary sovereignty and, usually, to illustrate how this has been affected by EU membership.

■ Sample question

Could you answer this question? Below is a typical problem question that could arise on this topic. Guidelines on answering the question are included at the end of this chapter, whilst a sample essay question and guidance on tackling it can be found on the companion website.

PROBLEM QUESTION

Warmsea is a south-coast seaside resort represented in Parliament by the fiercely patriotic Conservative Rodney Smith.

At his constituency surgery, Rodney sees Charlie Roper, owner of Glamcabs, the luxury taxi company which relies heavily for its income on the executives who visit the seafront conference centres which are central to Warmsea's economy. Having recently invested over £200,000 in a new fleet of luxury cars, Charlie is outraged to hear of an impending EU regulation imposing a 900cc maximum on engines in taxis as part of a policy of reducing emissions by public transport on environmental grounds. Faced with either selling his new fleet at a loss or paying for a costly engine conversion for each car, Charlie is determined to fight and is looking to his MP for support.

The following week, at Prime Minister's Questions, Rodney confronts the Prime Minister and asks him to ignore the regulation. In response he is told that the UK, as a member state of the EU, is obliged to implement EU provisions whatever the reservations of individual MPs, although the position would have been slightly different had this been a directive rather than a regulation. Rodney is far from satisfied by this answer and accuses the Prime Minister of cowardice. 'This is the British Parliament and we are supreme,' says Sir Rodney.

Is Rodney correct in his view?

Basic principles of the constitution

In considering how the constitution operates, there are a number of general themes or principles which must be recognised as exerting an influence. These include the so-called 'constitutional doctrines' of the **separation of powers**, the **rule of law** and **parliamentary sovereignty**, but there are also principles which are even more fundamental to how the state operates and these should also be considered.

Fundamental principles

Democracy

The UK is a democracy and the principle that those in power are in office because they have been elected is central to the operation of the state. The parliamentary process reflects the will of the people, who have elected their MPs to represent them and to pass legislation in their name. Similarly, it is the fact that the House of Lords has traditionally not been elected which has presented the greatest pressure for change.

Accountability

Closely linked to the principle of democracy is the requirement for accountability within the constitution. Those in power must be accountable for the way in which they use their powers, so that power cannot be abused. For example, civil servants are accountable to the minister who heads their department, and the minister is accountable to Parliament. In this way, much of the operation of the constitution is concerned with making sure that the mechanisms for ensuring accountability work properly.

Make your answer stand out

Demonstrate to the examiner that you can link various aspects of the subject together by mentioning that this emphasis on accountability has, to a degree, been undermined by a perceived weakening in the constitutional convention of ministerial responsibility which, theoretically, requires a minister to assume responsibility for the actions of their department.

■ Constitutional doctrines

The separation of powers

The doctrine of the separation of powers is a simple, but crucial, principle which underpins the way in which power is used by the state. Remember that originally all power was concentrated in the hands of the monarch, and consequently it was almost impossible to prevent the abuse of such power. For this reason, power within the modern constitution is divided between a number of key 'organs of state', which are considered in the next chapter. They oversee each other and have to work together to achieve their objectives. This serves either to prevent the abuse of power by any one part of the state, or at least to limit its impact.

The doctrine recognises that the division of power between the various organs of state is not always amicable and there are often tensions as one part of the state seeks to exert control over another. This is particularly true of the relationship between the executive and the courts.

The 'soft' separation of powers

The contrast is sometimes made between countries such as the USA, which are seen as having a very rigid separation of powers between the organs of the state, and the UK, where there is often said to be a 'soft' separation. All this means is that there is a little more flexibility in the UK system, which allows the various elements of the state to work together.

Composition and powers

Power in the UK is divided between the three organs of state: the **legislature**, the **executive** and the **judiciary**. Read Chapters 4–5 for more detail on each of these. It must be recognised that the powers of the monarch are now mostly symbolic.

Figure 3.1

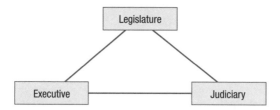

Overlapping personnel

It might be thought that a separation of powers requires different people to work within the three organs of state, but this is clearly not the case in the UK.

The Queen
Strictly speaking, the Queen is a member of all three organs of the state, with the concepts of 'the Queen's government', 'the Queen in Parliament' and 'the Queen's judges'. However,

within the modern constitution, the monarch is a largely symbolic presence which does not impact on the overall division of power within the state.

Ministers
A more important overlap is that of ministers who are members of the Cabinet (the executive) and also members of Parliament (the legislature). Note that it is not essential that a member of the Cabinet also be an MP, but most are.

KEY STATUTE

House of Commons Disqualification Act 1975, section 2

'Not more than ninety-five persons being the holders of offices specified in Schedule 2 to this Act (in this section referred to as Ministerial offices) shall be entitled to sit and vote in the House of Commons at any one time.'

Law Lords
Until 2009 the judges who sat in the Appellate Committee of the House of Lords, which was the highest court in the UK, were also members of the upper chamber of the legislature. This raised concerns over the effectiveness of the separation of powers in relation to this most important judicial function. The establishment of the Supreme Court, which replaced the House of Lords in 2009, was intended to remedy this situation, although the Law Lords who became the first Supreme Court Justices remain members of the House of Lords. All new Justices, however, will be directly appointed by a selection commission.

The Lord Chancellor
One of the most important changes in recent years has been to the role of the Lord Chancellor. Formerly, the Lord Chancellor was a member of all three organs of state, being a member of the Cabinet, Speaker of the House of Lords and head of the judiciary, but the powers of the Lord Chancellor were radically altered by the Constitutional Reform Act 2005 (CRA 2005).

The powers of the Lord Chancellor

	Legislative function	Executive function	Judicial function
Pre-CRA 2005	Speaker of the House of Lords	Member of the Cabinet	Head of Judiciary
			Appoints judges
Post-CRA 2005	Replaced by 'Lord Speaker'	Member of the Cabinet	Replaced as Head of Judiciary by Lord Chief Justice
			Judicial appointments now made by Judicial Appointments Commission

KEY STATUTE

Constitutional Reform Act 2005

The 2005 Act made a number of important changes to the constitution, including the creation of a Supreme Court. In relation to the Lord Chancellor, the Act replaced him as head of the judiciary with the Lord Chief Justice, and replaced him as Speaker of the House of Lords with the 'Lord Speaker'.

 Make your answer stand out

The changing role of the Lord Chancellor has been one of the most radical modifications to the constitution in recent years and has been the subject of heated debate. Many have argued that the Lord Chancellor fulfilled a vital role in communicating between the various organs of state, whereas others have suggested a political bias to the role. For a discussion of the key issues, see Woodhouse (2007).

The separation of powers in practice

The most important aspect of the separation of powers is the way in which the organs of state act to restrain each other and to prevent the other institutions from exceeding their powers.

KEY CASE

M v Home Office [1994] 1 AC 377

Concerning: accountability of the executive to the courts

Facts

M arrived in the UK from Zaire claiming political asylum, but his application was refused. The Home Secretary ordered his deportation but the High Court ordered the Home Secretary not to proceed with the deportation until the court had considered the case. The Home Secretary ignored the court order and M was deported.

Legal principle

The Home Secretary was held to be in contempt of court for refusing to comply with the order of the court. The fact that he was a minister of the Crown did not place him above the law and so the court could restrain him in the exercise of his powers. Lord Templeman: 'The argument that there is no power to enforce the law by injunction or contempt proceedings against a minister in his official capacity would, if upheld, establish the proposition that the executive obey the law as a matter of grace and not as a matter of necessity.'

KEY CASE

R v *Secretary of State for the Home Department, ex parte Anderson* [2003] 1 AC 837

Concerning: power to set life sentences

Facts

A was convicted of two murders and received the mandatory life sentence. The trial judge recommended that he serve at least 15 years, but the Home Secretary increased this to 20 years. The court had to consider whether the courts or the Home Secretary should set sentences for such prisoners.

Legal principle

It was for the courts and not the Home Secretary to set sentences. This was a judicial function and the involvement of a politician in the process contravened the right to a fair trial. Lord Steyn: 'The power of the Home Secretary in England and Wales to decide on the tariff to be served by mandatory life sentence prisoners is a striking anomaly in our legal system.'

KEY CASE

R v *Secretary of State for the Home Department, ex parte Fire Brigades Union* [1995] 2 AC 513

Concerning: power of the executive to ignore legislation

Facts

The Criminal Injuries Compensation Scheme operated under royal prerogative but was replaced by provisions of the Criminal Justice Act 1988, which allowed the Home Secretary to introduce a statutory scheme at a later date. Five years later, the Home Secretary had still not introduced the statutory compensation scheme and decided, instead, to amend the original scheme.

Legal principle

It was held that when an Act of Parliament allows a minister to decide when the provisions should come into force, this is not the same as allowing the minister to ignore the Act altogether. It is for Parliament to change the statute – not the minister. Lord Browne-Wilkinson: [the alternative would be] 'that both Houses of Parliament had passed the Bill through all its stages and the Act received the Royal Assent merely to confer an enabling power on the executive to decide at will whether or not to make the parliamentary provisions a part of the law'.

✎ EXAM TIP

In discussing the separation of powers, always emphasise the tensions which exist between the organs of state, particularly the judiciary and the executive. The separation of powers is not an amicable arrangement but rather a potential conflict, with each part of the state determined to retain its powers.

Make your answer stand out

Mention *R (on the application of Miller)* v *Secretary of State for Exiting the European Union* [2017] UKSC 5 (SC) which concerned the power of the government to trigger the Article 50 Brexit process. This case saw the courts reassert parliamentary sovereignty over the executive. See Chapter 11 for details.

The rule of law

The second constitutional doctrine is the rule of law, which can be a difficult principle to understand because there is not one simple 'rule' and there have been a number of different interpretations of the term. Basically, the rule of law is a set of underlying principles which governs how the legal system should operate and how the powers of the state should be controlled.

Exam answers on the rule of law are often weak and rambling. Impress the examiner by not only stating what the various definitions are but also by following this with some consideration of whether the various definitions appear to be reflected in our system. Even a relatively modest discussion will set your answer apart from the majority, which are simply descriptive.

 Don't be tempted to . . .

Defining the rule of law

Students frequently struggle to define the rule of law in their answers and this can lead to confusion. Being vague on this point will make the examiner wonder if you understand the concept at all, so make reference to some of the following definitions to demonstrate your understanding of what the term is taken to mean.

Definitions of the rule of law

Writer	Key features
Joseph Raz (1979)	Law should be general, open and clear
	Law should be stable
	Judiciary should be independent
	Law should not be biased
	Courts able to review state powers
	Courts should be accessible

Writer	Key features
'Declaration of Delhi' (1959)	Representative government
	No retrospective law
	Respect for human rights
	The right to challenge the state
	Right to a fair trial
Albert Dicey (1885)	No arbitrary power
	State power should be specified in law
	No punishment except for breach of the law
	Law applies to all persons equally

A more recent and comprehensive definition of the doctrine was provided by Lord Bingham in his 2011 book *The Rule of Law*. Here he sets out the following principles:

1. The law must be accessible, intelligible, clear and predictable.
2. Questions of legal right and liability should ordinarily be resolved by the exercise of the law and not the exercise of discretion.
3. Laws should apply equally to all.
4. Ministers and public officials must exercise the powers conferred in good faith, fairly, for the purposes for which they were conferred – reasonably and without exceeding the limits of such powers.
5. The law must afford adequate protection of fundamental human rights.
6. The state must provide a way of resolving disputes which the parties cannot themselves resolve.
7. The adjudicative procedures provided by the state should be fair.
8. The rule of law requires compliance by the state with its obligations in international as well as national laws.

Main principles

The most important common principle in the above definitions is that no one should be above the law, including the government, and that the state should only be able to act in accordance with the law and not in an arbitrary way (i.e. as it sees fit).

KEY CASE

Entick v *Carrington* (1765) 19 State Tr 1029 (Ct of CP)

Concerning: the limits of state powers

Facts

The king's messengers broke into Entick's house on orders from the Secretary of State to seize both Entick and his papers (he was suspected of treason). Entick challenged the legality of the search but the Secretary of State argued that such powers were an essential part of government.

Legal principle

The state had to act within legal authority. Therefore, if there was no statute or common law precedent which authorised the search, it would be illegal. The state was not above the law. Lord Camden CJ: 'If this was law it would be found in our books, but no such law ever existed in this country.'

KEY CASE

Antoine v *Sharma* [2007] 1 WLR 780, Lord Bingham

Concerning: the rule of law

Facts

To avoid prosecution on a charge of attempting to pervert the course of public justice, the Chief Justice of Trinidad and Tobago sought judicial review of the decision to prosecute and an order staying all action consequential on that decision. The decision for the court was whether to permit judicial review of the decision to prosecute or whether to allow the ordinary criminal process to take its course.

Legal principle

Lord Bingham: 'The rule of law requires that, subject to any immunity or exemption provided by law, the criminal law of the land should apply to all alike. A person is not to be singled out for adverse treatment because he or she holds a high and dignified office of State, but nor can the holding of such an office excuse conduct which would lead to the prosecution of one not holding such an office. The maintenance of public confidence in the administration of justice requires that it be, and be seen to be, even-handed.'

This represents the general position, but that is not to say that all are treated equally before the law, and there are a number of recognised exceptions to this principle. The most notable of these is the diplomatic immunity from prosecution afforded to foreign diplomatic personnel under the Vienna Convention on Diplomatic Relations 1961.

KEY INSTRUMENT

Vienna Convention on Diplomatic Relations 1961, Article 29

'The person of a diplomatic agent shall be inviolable. He shall not be liable to any form of arrest or detention. The receiving State shall treat him with due respect and shall take all appropriate steps to prevent any attack on his person, freedom or dignity.'

Parliamentary sovereignty

Of all the constitutional doctrines, parliamentary sovereignty is the most fundamental principle guiding the operation of the state and it draws on the themes of democracy and accountability mentioned earlier. Put simply, the doctrine states that Parliament is the supreme body within the constitution.

 Make your answer stand out

Parliamentary sovereignty is a popular topic for examiners and it is possible to score high marks with a structured approach. Remember that examiners will frequently be looking not only for a basic overview of the doctrine itself but also for some discussion of how it has been undermined by membership of the EU. Always read the question carefully to determine where the examiner wants you to place the emphasis in your answer – on the domestic or the EU dimension. Also, remember to include as many examples as possible from statute and case law – this will make your answer really stand out!

! Don't be tempted to . . .

Parliamentary sovereignty and the separation of powers

There is potential for confusion when considering parliamentary sovereignty and the separation of powers. The separation of powers seems to suggest that the organs of the state can oversee each other to prevent the abuse of power, but parliamentary sovereignty allows Parliament to override any other part of the state. The simplest way to approach this is to remember that, ultimately, one body has to have control to prevent deadlock, and that in a democracy that should be the elected body – Parliament.

3 BASIC PRINCIPLES OF THE CONSTITUTION

Definition of sovereignty

The most commonly applied definition of parliamentary sovereignty comes from Dicey, who suggested three key rules:

1 Parliament can make or unmake any law

If there were areas of law which Parliament could not change then that would suggest that someone was telling Parliament what to do and, therefore, that Parliament was not sovereign.

KEY STATUTE

His Majesty's Declaration of Abdication Act 1936

In 1936 King Edward VIII wished to marry American divorcee Wallis Simpson, causing a constitutional crisis, as it was widely believed that the country would not accept Simpson as its queen. In order to marry, Edward gave up the throne, but this required an Act of Parliament in order to take effect. In this way, the monarch could not act without the agreement of Parliament.

KEY STATUTE

Union with Ireland Act 1800

This united England and Ireland. In this way, Parliament was able to alter the physical limits of the state and the land which it covered, bringing the people of Ireland under the sovereignty of Parliament.

KEY STATUTE

Parliament Act 1911

In 1909 the House of Lords refused to pass the budget approved by the House of Commons. This was seen as the unelected Lords challenging the elected Commons, and so Parliament introduced the 1911 Act to restrict the power of the Lords to delay legislation. In this way, Parliament was able to legislate over its own procedures and the way in which the law is made.

KEY CASE

Jackson and others v *Attorney General* [2005] UKHL 56 (HL)

Concerning: the Parliament Act 1911 and 1949

Facts

The appellants argued that the 2004 Hunting Act, which effectively banned foxhunting, was invalid as it had been passed in accordance with the provisions of the 1949 Parliament Act which was itself passed in accordance with the 1911 Act. It was claimed that provisions implemented under the powers of the 1911 Act were subordinate, rather than primary, legislation and so could not be used to introduce valid Acts of Parliament such as the 2004 Act.

Legal principle

Held – Lord Bingham: 'The Parliament Act 1911 spells out when it may be used and what must be done in order to legislate under it. Parliament as ordinarily constituted enacted the 1911 Act. Acting in accordance with the conditions appearing on the face of the 1911 Act Parliament as redefined in that Act . . . enacted the Parliament Act 1949. Prima facie the Parliament Act 1949 is valid.'

2 Parliament cannot bind its successors

Because it is the institution of Parliament which is sovereign, each successive Parliament can change the legislation passed by previous Parliaments. This means that the 2009 Parliament can change legislation made by the 2008 Parliament. Similarly, the 2009 Parliament cannot pass a statute which could not be changed by the 2010 Parliament. If this were not the case then there would be areas of law which Parliament could not affect, which would break Dicey's first rule.

KEY STATUTE

Ireland Act 1949

In 1800 Parliament passed the Union with Ireland Act, which stated that England and Ireland should, 'from the first day of January . . . and for ever after, be united into one kingdom'. In 1949 Parliament granted Ireland its independence from England. The fact that the 1800 Parliament had intended a 'permanent' union did not prevent Parliament from passing the later Act.

This raises the 'doctrine of implied repeal', which states that if an Act of Parliament is inconsistent with an earlier statute, the later Act is taken to repeal the first.

KEY CASE

Vauxhall Estates Ltd v Liverpool Corporation [1932] 1 KB 733 (DC)

Concerning: the doctrine of implied repeal

Facts

The corporation took the plaintiff's property under a compulsory purchase order. In calculating the compensation to be paid, the corporation wanted to rely on the terms of the Housing Act 1925, but the plaintiff argued that the calculation should be based on the (more generous) terms of the Acquisition of Land (Assessment of Compensation) Act 1919.

Legal principle

It was held that the provisions of the later Act should apply. Avory J: 'I am unable to understand why Parliament should not have power impliedly to repeal or impliedly to amend these provisions [of the 1919 Act] by the mere enactment of provisions completely inconsistent with them.'

3 No one can question Parliament's laws

Although the rule speaks of 'no one', the key issue is whether the courts can challenge Parliament. Under the traditional model of parliamentary sovereignty, the answer is 'no'.

KEY CASE

British Railways Board v Pickin [1974] AC 765 (HL)

Concerning: the power of the court to challenge Parliament

Facts

P sought to challenge the British Railways Act 1968, arguing that the statute was invalid as there were irregularities in the procedure which had led to it being passed.

Legal principle

It was held that it was not for the court to examine how an Act of Parliament had come into force or to question the correctness of the procedures employed within Parliament. If the statute had been passed by Parliament, the role of the court was simply to apply the provisions. Lord Reid: 'The function of the court is to construe and apply the enactments of Parliament. The court has no concern with the manner in which Parliament or its officers . . . perform these functions.'

Parliamentary sovereignty and EU law

Having established that Dicey's rules apply, we need to consider the impact of our membership of the EU on parliamentary sovereignty.

Don't be tempted to . . .

Parliamentary sovereignty and the EU

Membership of the EU has had a dramatic effect on parliamentary sovereignty, so you must be prepared to include reference to this in your answer, depending on whether the question raises this issue. This will require reference to specific provisions and cases if you are to achieve a high mark.

✓ Make your answer stand out

When discussing parliamentary sovereignty, illustrate that you are aware of recent political developments by indicating the complications posed by increasing powers devolved to Scotland, Wales and Northern Ireland.

KEY STATUTE

European Communities Act 1972, section 2

General implementation of Treaties

(1) All such rights, powers, liabilities, obligations and restrictions from time to time created or arising by or under the Treaties . . . are without further enactment to be given legal effect or used in the United Kingdom shall be recognised and available in law, and be enforced, allowed and followed accordingly

[The reference to 'without further enactment' is crucial, as this means without Parliament.]

Regulations and directives

EU provisions implemented in the form of regulations or directives also have implications for parliamentary sovereignty. In particular, because regulations are 'directly applicable', they do not require an Act of Parliament to come into force, thereby further undermining parliamentary sovereignty.

Type of provision	Features
Regulation	General in application (applies to all member states)
	Binding in its entirety
	Directly applicable (requires no Act of Parliament to take effect)
Directive	Specific in application (applies only to certain member states)
	Binding as to the result to be achieved
	Not directly applicable (requires an Act of Parliament to take effect)

KEY CASE

R v Secretary of State for Transport, ex parte Factortame Ltd (No. 2) **[1991] 1 AC 603 (HL)**

Concerning: the supremacy of EU over UK law

Facts

Spanish fishermen sought to avoid fishing quotas by registering their ships in the UK, allowing them to take fish under part of the UK quota as well. The government introduced legislation to prevent this, by requiring ships registered in the UK to be 75% owned by 'qualified persons' who were British citizens resident in the UK, but the fishermen argued that such measures were contrary to EU law.

Legal principle

It was held that, where there was conflict between EU and domestic law, the courts must give effect to the EU provisions. The law of Parliament could be set aside. Lord Bridge: 'It has always been clear that it was the duty of a United Kingdom court, when delivering final judgment, to override any rule of national law found to be in conflict with any directly enforceable rule of Community law.'

KEY CASE

Francovich v Italy **Case C-9/90 [1995] ICR 722, Mischo, AG**

Concerning: non-implementation of EU directives

Facts

The Italian state failed to implement an EU directive which ensured that employees of insolvent companies would be paid wages owed to them.

Legal principle

It was held that, as the Italian state had failed in its obligation to implement the directive, it must compensate individuals who had suffered loss as a consequence. Mischo, AG: 'Individuals must be entitled to bring proceedings against a member state before the national courts for compensation for harm caused to them by the failure to implement the provisions of Directive 80/987.'

Parliamentary sovereignty and the Human Rights Act 1998 (HRA)

Another important question surrounds the extent to which the Human Rights Act 1998, which permits the courts to make a declaration of incompatibility in relation to domestic statute, represents an erosion of parliamentary sovereignty. Here the position was clarified by the House of Lords.

KEY CASE

R v Secretary of State for the Home Department, ex parte Simms **[1999] UKHL 33 (HL)**

Concerning: parliamentary sovereignty

Facts

In a case decided following the passing of the HRA 1998 but before it came into force, the court was required to consider whether restricting a prisoner's right to communicate with a journalist was an unlawful interference with the right of freedom of speech.

Legal principle

In ruling that the policy of the Secretary of State in imposing an indiscriminate ban on such interviews was unlawful, Lord Hoffmann stated: '*Parliamentary sovereignty* means that Parliament can, if it chooses, legislate contrary to fundamental principles of human rights. The Human Rights Act 1998 will not detract from this power. The constraints upon its exercise by Parliament are ultimately political, not legal.'

■ Putting it all together

Answer guidelines

See the problem question at the start of the chapter.

Approaching the question

- Address the question in two parts – first, establish the principle of parliamentary sovereignty; second, set out the impact of EU membership on the doctrine.

Important points to include

- Remember that the examiner wants to see both description and analysis in your answer. This means that you should set out the relevant law clearly before moving on to offer some application. In this way, a good answer to this question will first explain how parliamentary sovereignty works and then illustrate how EU membership has eroded the doctrine.

- Begin by setting out the principle of parliamentary sovereignty, making reference to Dicey's three tests. Provide examples of each and show how they contribute to the overall proposition that Parliament is supreme within the constitution.

- Then address the scenario, which requires you to consider EU regulations and directives. Explain the impact of the European Communities Act 1972 and the decision in *Factortame,* before highlighting the difference between regulations and directives (that regulations are directly applicable and so become part of UK law without Parliament, whereas directives require an Act of Parliament to take effect).

- Conclude that there is little scope for the Prime Minister and the government to avoid their obligations under EU law and little scope for Parliament to challenge its provisions.

 Make your answer stand out

- Mention that, even in the case of directives, the UK government could be sued in the European Court for failing to implement the provisions of a directive, following the decision in *Francovich* v *Italy* (1991).

- Point out that, although the government is bound to follow EU law, which undermines parliamentary sovereignty, this is only because Parliament enacted the European Communities Act 1972. Under Dicey's tests, Parliament could repeal the Act at any time, thereby removing the UK from the EU and regaining sovereignty. For political and economic reasons this is very unlikely to happen, but it *is* possible, and the examiner will give you credit for recognising this point.

READ TO IMPRESS

Barber, N.W. (2011) The afterlife of parliamentary sovereignty. *International Journal of Constitutional Law*, 9(1): 144–54.

Bingham, T. (2011) *The Rule of Law*. London: Penguin.

Barendt, E. (1995) Separation of powers and constitutional government. *Public Law*, 599–619.

Craig, P.P. (1997) Formal and substantive conceptions of the rule of law: an analytical framework. *Public Law*, 467–87.

Dicey, A.V. (1885) *An Introduction to the Study of the Constitution*, 10th edn (1959). London: Macmillan.

Elliott, M. (1999) The demise of parliamentary sovereignty? The implications for justifying judicial review. *Law Quarterly Review*, 115: 119–37.

Elliott, M. (2004) Parliamentary sovereignty under pressure. *International Journal of Constitutional Law*, 2: 545–627.

Griffith, J.A.G. (2001) The common law and the political constitution. *Law Quarterly Review*, 117: 42–67.

Jowell, J. (2006) Parliamentary sovereignty under the new constitutional hypothesis. *Public Law*, 562–80.

Lakin, S. (2008) Debunking the idea of parliamentary sovereignty: the controlling factor of legality in the British constitution. *Oxford Journal of Legal Studies*, 28: 709–34.

Raz, J. (1979) *The Authority of Law: Essays on Law and Morality*. Oxford: Oxford University Press.

Tucker, A. (2011) Uncertainty in the rule of recognition and in the doctrine of parliamentary sovereignty. *Oxford Journal of Legal Studies*, 31(1): 61–88.

Williams, D. (2000) Bias, judges and the separation of powers. *Public Law*, 45–60.

Woodhouse, D. (2007) The Constitutional Reform Act 2005: defending judicial independence the English way. *International Journal of Constitutional Law*, 5: 153–65.

www.pearsoned.co.uk/lawexpress

 Go online to access more revision support including quizzes to test your knowledge, sample questions with answer guidelines, printable versions of the topic maps, and more!

Institutions of state 1

Revision checklist

Essential points you should know:

- ☐ The constitutional position of the monarch as a head of state who retains largely symbolic powers in relation to the operation of the state
- ☐ The importance within the constitution of the independent judiciary which can act to protect the individual from abuse of state powers
- ☐ The function and forms of contempt of court as a means of ensuring the administration of justice
- ☐ The composition and function of the executive and the relationship between the state and its ministers (including the process of devolution)
- ☐ The development of ministerial responsibility as a constitutional convention

■ Topic map

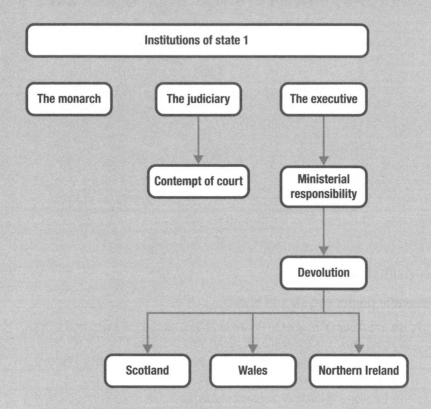

A printable version of this topic map is available from **www.pearsoned.co.uk/lawexpress**

■ Introduction

The 'state' comprises a number of institutions which have to work together.

There are a number of institutions which make up the 'state' and which use the powers given to them under the separation of powers discussed in Chapter 3. You need to understand their different functions within the constitution, and examiners will want to see that you can identify how they work together. Over the centuries, power has shifted from the monarch to the other institutions of state, and students need to be clear on where power lies within 'the system'. You also need to understand the role of both contempt of court and ministerial responsibility as mechanisms which contribute (in very different ways) to the operation of the state.

ASSESSMENT ADVICE

Essay questions

Essay questions might involve consideration of how ultimate power within the constitution has shifted from the monarch to the other institutions of state. You may also be asked to explore the operation of government and the relationship between Prime Minister, ministers and civil servants – possibly within the context of ministerial responsibility. In all cases, the examiner will be looking for both an understanding of the composition and function of the various state institutions, and an appreciation of the relative strengths and weaknesses of the system. Therefore, description must be accompanied by analysis and criticism.

Problem questions

Problem questions on contempt of court or ministerial responsibility are common and, in both cases, examiners will be looking for an appreciation of how the law has changed. Questions on contempt of court will usually centre on the impact of the Contempt of Court Act 1981 and questions on ministerial responsibility will be looking for discussion of the changing nature of this constitutional convention. As with other areas, the best answers will utilise examples to support their arguments.

■ Sample question

Could you answer this question? Below is a typical problem question that could arise on this topic. Guidelines on answering the question are included at the end of this chapter, whilst a sample essay question and guidance on tackling it can be found on the companion website.

PROBLEM QUESTION

Roland Dutton is a senior civil servant in the Department of Transport, with responsibility for the introduction of a new computerised ticketing system for the London Underground. Determined to make a name for himself with this high-profile project, he refuses all offers of assistance and delivers the project on time, largely by cutting corners during the testing programme. His minister, George Shaw, is kept informed in general terms but takes little real interest in the detailed progress of the project. Cobb, who is a colleague of Dutton, warns the minister that the testing programme appears superficial, but he is ignored. The introduction of the new system is a disaster, with the entire underground network gridlocked for a week. The cost to the economy is estimated in billions and seven people are trampled to death in the confusion of overcrowded tube stations.

The minister is called to the House to explain the fiasco, and the Transport Select Committee calls both Dutton and Cobb to explain their role in the development of the system. Prior to appearing before the Committee, Cobb is summoned by the minister and told that he should make no mention of his earlier warning when giving evidence.

There is growing pressure on George Shaw to resign over the issue, but the minister refuses, stating that there is no precedent for him to resign over such a matter and that, in any event, this is merely an operational mistake for which he cannot and should not be held responsible.

Discuss.

The monarch

Although the UK is a parliamentary democracy, it retains a monarch as head of state. As such, the monarch presides over events such as the state opening of Parliament, and acts as host to foreign heads of state when they visit the UK. What has changed over the past 300 years, however, is the extent of the real power exercised by the monarch within the constitution.

REVISION NOTE

Although you are highly unlikely to face an exam question solely on the monarch, it is a subject which features in many possible exam questions, as part of topics such as the royal prerogative, the separation of powers and parliamentary sovereignty. The diminishing powers of the monarch is one of the most important themes underpinning the development of the modern constitution, so examiners will give credit for mention of this as part of the discussion.

Centuries ago, all power within the state was in the hands of the monarch. Now, because of parliamentary sovereignty and the separation of powers, most of the power originally exercised by the monarch lies elsewhere. That is not to say, however, that the monarch is unimportant.

The monarch is currently:

- Head of state
- Head of the Commonwealth
- Head of the Church of England
- Commander-in-Chief of the Armed Forces.

In addition, the monarch has the following powers:

- summoning and dissolving Parliament
- appointing the Prime Minister
- appointing ministers (following the advice of the Prime Minister)
- declaring war.

The judiciary

The next key institution of state is the **judiciary**. Although the term technically covers all judges, it is those who sit in the higher courts (most obviously the Supreme Court) who are most important to the operation of the constitution, as they are in a position to challenge the government and ensure that it functions within the law.

The independent judiciary

The constitution of the UK places great emphasis on the independence of the judiciary – i.e. that it is not influenced or controlled by the government of the day. Only if the judiciary is free from such control can it act in the best interests of the people and hold the government to account where it exceeds its powers. Factors which emphasise this independence include:

- Judges cannot be sued. They are immune from liability for the decisions they reach.
- By convention, ministers will not criticise judges or the decisions they reach in particular cases.
- Ministers and MPs will not comment on cases currently before the courts (also known as *sub judice*).
- Judges must not actively participate in politics.
- Senior judges (High Court, Court of Appeal and Supreme Court) cannot be removed from office without a resolution passed by both Houses of Parliament.

EXAM TIP

Emphasise the importance of an independent judiciary and the way in which the government relies on this. Public inquiries, such as those into the Hillsborough disaster, 'Bloody Sunday' or the Hatfield rail crash, are always chaired by a senior judge to emphasise the independence of the proceedings. A more recent example is the inquiry chaired by Lord Justice Leveson into the culture, practice and ethics of journalists.

Contempt of court

The law prohibits actions which bring the administration of justice into disrepute. This falls under the heading of 'contempt of court', which can be either civil or criminal.

Civil contempt	Criminal contempt
Refusal to obey an order of the court	Scandalising the court (attacks on the impartiality or integrity of a judge)
	Contempt in the face of the court
	Publication prejudicial to the course of justice

KEY CASE

R v *New Statesman (Editor), ex parte DPP [1928] 44 TLR 301 (KBD)*

Concerning: scandalising the court

Facts

The *New Statesman* magazine published an article in which it was stated: 'an individual owning to such views . . . cannot apparently hope for a fair hearing in a court presided over by Mr Justice Avory'.

Legal principle

It was held that this brought the integrity of the judge into disrepute and so constituted a contempt of court.

KEY CASE

Morris v *Crown Office [1970] 2 QB 114 (CA)*

Concerning: contempt in the face of the court

Facts

A group of students disrupted a sitting of the High Court by singing and shouting slogans.

Legal principle

The judge instantly sentenced the ringleaders to three months' imprisonment. The power to do so was upheld on appeal. Salmon, LJ: 'The law of contempt is not for the protection of the judge but for that of the administration of justice.'

KEY CASE

Sunday Times v United Kingdom [1979] 2 EHRR 245 (ECHR)

Concerning: publications prejudicial to the course of justice

Facts

The Sunday Times was prevented by injunction from publishing an article on the Thalidomide drug scandal at a time when the parties to the case were engaged in negotiations to reach a settlement.

Legal principle

The case went to the European Court of Human Rights, where the UK law was found to breach Article 10 (right to freedom of expression). Zekia, J: 'The branch of the common law that concerns contempt of court dealing with publications in the press and other media in connection with pending civil proceedings was – at any rate on the material date – uncertain and unsettled – and unascertainable even by a qualified lawyer.' This led to the passage of the Contempt of Court Act 1981.

Contempt of Court Act 1981

Note that the law on publications by newspapers, etc. is now governed by the Contempt of Court Act 1981, which operates on the basis of 'strict liability'.

KEY STATUTE

Contempt of Court Act 1981, section 1

The strict liability rule

In this Act, 'the strict liability rule' means the rule of law whereby conduct may be treated as a contempt of court tending to interfere with the course of justice, in particular legal proceedings, regardless of intent to do so.

Contempt of Court Act 1981, section 2

Limitation of scope of strict liability

1. The strict liability rule applies only in relation to publications, and for this purpose 'publication' includes any speech, writing, [programme included in a programme

service] or other communication in whatever form, which is addressed to the public at large or any section of the public.

2. The strict liability rule applies only to a publication which creates a substantial risk that the course of justice in the proceedings in question will be seriously impeded or prejudiced.

3. The strict liability rule applies to a publication only if the proceedings in question are active within the meaning of this section at the time of the publication.

Increasingly, contempt of court cases feature the misuse of social media to circumvent an order of the court and this is likely to become more common in the future.

KEY CASE

Attorney General v Hawkins; Attorney General v Liddle [2013] EWHC 1455 (Admin) (DC)

Concerning: contempt of court

Facts

The defendants separately posted photographs on Twitter and Facebook purporting to be of Jon Venables and Robert Thompson, the killers of Jamie Bulger. This was in breach of the 2001 lifetime injunction prohibiting publication of any details of the new identities given to the pair on their release from custody. The defendants received suspended sentences.

Legal principle

Sir John Thomas: 'We must also take into account the very serious nature of publication on a social media or otherwise on the internet . . . [which] can reach very many people, as this case shows. Therefore the conduct of anyone who publishes such information, whether it be on the social media or elsewhere on the internet, has that very serious consequence.'

KEY CASE

Attorney General v Dallas [2012] EWHC 156 (Admin) (AC)

Concerning: contempt of court

Facts

During the course of a trial, one of the jurors conducted an internet search to determine whether the accused had any previous convictions. This was in direct contravention of instructions given to the jury by the judge at the start of the trial.

Legal principle

The juror received a sentence of three months' imprisonment. Lord Judge CJ: 'Misuse of the internet by a juror is always a most serious irregularity, and an effective custodial sentence is virtually inevitable. The objective of such a sentence is to ensure that the integrity of the process of trial by jury is sustained.'

■ The executive

The definition of an 'executive' is a body which formulates and implements policy. In the study of constitutional and administrative law, however, the term is generally used to mean central government. The way in which the executive operates and interacts with the other institutions of state is a crucial aspect of the study of the constitution.

The Prime Minister

The executive is led by the Prime Minister, who is responsible for the overall conduct of the government and for the appointment of the ministers who head each of the departments (transport, health, defence, etc.).

The Cabinet

The Cabinet comprises the ministers who head each of the departments (Secretaries of State) together with ministers responsible for government business in the Commons (Leader of the House) and the Lords (Lord Privy Seal).

Ministers

Each department has a minister who takes responsibility for the way in which the department functions and the extent to which it achieves its objectives.

Ministerial responsibility

Ministers are bound by two constitutional conventions which fall under the heading 'ministerial responsibility'.

! Don't be tempted to . . .

Examples of ministerial responsibility

Because ministerial responsibility is a constitutional convention, it is a 'non-legal' rule and so not enforced by the courts. This means that examples are not decided cases but are simply 'political events'. Don't make the mistake of discussing such examples as if they were decisions of the court.

Collective ministerial responsibility

When a decision is reached by the Cabinet, all ministers must publicly support that decision, even if they opposed it during the Cabinet discussions. If a minister cannot do this, then they must resign from the government. This is important for the effective working of the executive as it enables the government to present a 'united front' around clear and agreed policies. If ministers were seen to disagree with each other over key policies, this would undermine public confidence in the authority of the government and the Prime Minister.

✎ EXAM TIP

When discussing collective responsibility, make sure to point out that the shadow cabinet is also subject to this principle, so that they too portray a 'united front'. Also emphasise that the doctrine applies only to the 'front bench' of each party (i.e. ministers and 'shadow' ministers); the 'backbench' MPs are not bound by the doctrine and so can disagree with their party if they so wish.

KEY ISSUE

NHS charges

Concerning: collective ministerial responsibility

Facts

Faced with the cost of the new National Health Service, which had been intended to be free for all, the government decided to impose charges for some services. Three ministers – Aneurin Bevan, John Freeman and Harold Wilson – resigned.

Principle

A minister who cannot stand by the decision of the government in public cannot retain their post.

KEY ISSUE

The 'Westland affair'

Concerning: collective ministerial responsibility

Facts

The UK's last military helicopter company was for sale. The Prime Minister, Margaret Thatcher, favoured a US buyer, but the Defence Secretary, Michael Heseltine, favoured a European bid. Heseltine was outvoted and resigned from the Cabinet, as he felt he could not publicly support the decision.

Principle

A minister who cannot stand by the decision of the government in public cannot retain their post.

Make your answer stand out

Point out that the then Prime Minister, David Cameron, relaxed the rules on collective responsibility during the EU referendum campaign. This allowed his ministers to campaign for whichever side they wished although, with hindsight, he may well wish that he hadn't.

Individual ministerial responsibility

Each government department has many thousands of civil servants working within it. Such civil servants are not directly accountable to Parliament as it is the minister who must explain the operation of the department. In this way, if there is a serious error within the department, it is the minister who should assume 'individual ministerial responsibility' and, ultimately, resign. The convention has changed dramatically over the years, so that now it is highly unusual for a minister to resign because of failings within their department.

KEY ISSUE

The 'Crichel Down affair'

Concerning: individual ministerial responsibility

Facts

A plot of land which had been requisitioned by the army during the Second World War was transferred to the Ministry of Agriculture after the war. The original owners of part of the land wished to reclaim it, but their claim was mishandled by the Ministry. As a result, the minister, Thomas Dugdale, resigned.

Principle

This is generally seen as the 'classic' example of individual ministerial responsibility. Dugdale was in charge of the department and so felt obliged to resign.

Examples of individual ministerial responsibility resignations after Crichel Down

Lord Carrington (1982)	Resigned over the invasion of the Falkland Islands (his staff failed to predict the invasion)
Leon Brittan (1986)	Resigned in the aftermath of the Westland affair (his staff leaked a letter from the Attorney General to the press)
Stephen Byers (2002)	Resigned after allegations of misleading Parliament over the failure of Railtrack, the company set up to manage the UK rail network

There are, however, many more ministers who have held on to their jobs despite widespread calls for them to resign.

Examples of individual ministerial responsibility non-resignations

William Whitelaw (1982)	Faced calls for his resignation after an intruder reached the Queen's bedroom
James Prior (1984)	Faced calls for his resignation after mass escape from the Maze Prison in Belfast
Michael Howard (1995)	Faced calls for his resignation over mass prison escapes

 Don't be tempted to . . .

Personal resignations

When considering the question of ministerial resignations, be careful not to include those resignations which have followed 'personal indiscretion', such as the resignations of Cecil Parkinson, Tim Yeo, David Blunkett and Peter Mandelson. In these cases, ministers resigned because their personal conduct raised questions over their integrity, not because of errors within their departments. Therefore, these are not examples of ministerial responsibility.

Why do ministers lose their jobs?

Remember that a minister's chances of holding on to their job owe more to political circumstances than to the facts of the case. In this way, factors which influence a minister's chances include:

- Is Parliament sitting? (A scandal during the summer break is less likely to result in a resignation as MPs are not in Parliament to create pressure on the minister)
- Personal popularity with the Prime Minister
- Popularity with the party
- World events (the media are easily distracted by a disaster or other 'big story').

 Make your answer stand out

The changing nature of the convention of ministerial responsibility is a key area of change within the constitution, and examiners will give credit for a broader understanding of the debate. By considering the reasons why ministers are far less likely to resign than in the past, it is possible to demonstrate precisely the analytical skills which examiners are looking for. Read Bamforth (2005) for an overview of the issues.

Devolution

Another key aspect of the executive is the shift under the current government towards **devolution**.

KEY DEFINITION: Devolution

The process by which power is given by (or 'devolved' from) Westminster to Scotland, Wales and Northern Ireland, giving them greater control over their own affairs and the power to make their own laws in certain areas. This is not full independence, however, as Westminster retains power over key areas such as defence.

Scotland   The Scotland Act 1998 created the Scottish executive and the Scottish Parliament. It has devolved powers over a number of areas including:

- agriculture, forestry and fisheries
- education and training
- environment
- health and social services
- housing
- law and order
- local government
- sport and the arts
- tourism and economic development
- many aspects of transport.

However, Westminster retains power over areas such as:

- benefits and social security
- immigration
- defence
- foreign policy
- employment
- broadcasting
- trade and industry
- nuclear energy, oil, coal, gas and electricity
- consumer rights
- data protection
- the constitution.

Wales   The Government of Wales Act 1998 created the Welsh Assembly, which has fewer powers than the Scottish Parliament but can pass laws (known as Assembly Acts), although only in areas where those powers have been expressly conferred. These powers are outlined in Schedule 7 to the Government of Wales Act 2006, as follows:

- Agriculture, Forestry, Animals, Plants and Rural Development
- Ancient Monuments and Historic Buildings
- Culture
- Economic Development
- Education and Training
- Environment
- Fire and Rescue Services and Fire Safety
- Food
- Health and Health Services
- Highways and Transport
- Housing
- Local Government
- National Assembly for Wales
- Public Administration
- Social Welfare
- Sport and Recreation
- Tourism
- Town and Country Planning
- Water and Flood Defence
- Welsh Language.

Other areas remain under the control of Westminster.

Northern Ireland   The Northern Ireland Assembly was created by the 1998 'Belfast Agreement' (also known as the 'Good Friday Agreement'). The Assembly has been suspended a number of times, but came back into power in May 2007. The Northern Ireland Assembly has full legislative powers in the following areas:

- health and social services
- education
- employment and skills
- agriculture
- social security
- pensions and child support
- housing
- economic development
- local government
- environmental issues, including planning

- transport
- culture and sport
- the Northern Ireland Civil Service
- equal opportunities
- justice and policing.

The UK government retains responsibility for:

- the constitution
- royal succession
- international relations
- defence and armed forces
- nationality, immigration and asylum
- elections
- national security
- nuclear energy
- UK-wide taxation
- currency
- conferring of honours
- international treaties.

In addition, there are a number of 'reserved matters' where legislative authority generally rests with Westminster, but where the Northern Ireland Assembly can legislate with the consent of the Secretary of State for Northern Ireland. These include:

- firearms and explosives
- financial services and pensions regulation
- broadcasting
- import and export controls
- navigation and civil aviation
- international trade and financial markets
- telecommunications and postage
- the foreshore and seabed
- disqualification from Assembly membership
- consumer safety
- intellectual property.

Although the process of devolution should be the same for Scotland, Wales and Northern Ireland, the result has been very different. Scotland has significantly more power over its own affairs than Wales, and the process in Northern Ireland has been dogged by delay and argument between the political parties as a legacy of the historical conflict within the province.

Make your answer stand out

The examiner will want to see that you are up to date with recent developments, so, in discussing devolution in Northern Ireland, mention the crisis caused by the alliance between the Democratic Unionist Party (DUP) and the British Conservative Party which has allowed the latter to remain in power despite losing their overall majority in the 2017 general election. Many have argued that this alliance contravenes the commitment of the UK government to remain impartial between Unionists and Nationalists in Northern Ireland.

Also, make clear that the border between Northern Ireland (which is part of the UK) and Southern Ireland is now a key issue in the Brexit negotiations, with many fearing the return of a 'hard' border between the two countries.

Scottish independence

The position in relation to Scotland has become increasingly contentious in the aftermath of both the referendum on Scottish independence in September 2014, which saw a 55% to 45% vote in favour of remaining within the UK, and the 2015 general election, which saw the Scottish National Party take 56 of the 59 Scottish parliamentary seats. This effectively removed the Labour and Conservative parties from Scotland and has raised serious questions about the legitimacy of the Westminster Parliament continuing to legislate over Scotland. The result has been renewed calls for a second referendum on full Scottish independence.

 Make your answer stand out

Point out that calls for Scottish independence increased in the aftermath of the EU referendum, as the majority of Scottish voters indicated that they wished to remain within the EU.

■ Putting it all together

Answer guidelines

See the problem question at the start of the chapter.

Approaching the question

■ Adopt a simple structure for your answer. Make sure you provide clear definitions of both collective and individual ministerial responsibility before considering the issues raised by the scenario.

Important points to include

■ Do not jump straight to individual ministerial responsibility – take some time to outline the nature of collective responsibility as well.

■ Point out that it is the minister and not the civil servant who is accountable to Parliament.

■ The central issue is the degree to which the minister should accept responsibility for the actions of Dutton. It might be argued that the minister was unaware of Dutton's activities (which would tend to undermine arguments for his resignation), but he was informed by Cobb and this would tend to undermine the minister's position.

■ The pressure placed on Cobb to lie to Parliament is extremely serious. Misleading Parliament has prompted resignations in the past.

 Make your answer stand out

Include examples from recent history. Remember, because ministerial responsibility is a convention, there are no decided cases, but you should use examples to illustrate your points. All too often, students forget to use such examples and this greatly undermines their answers.

READ TO IMPRESS

Bamforth, N. (2005) Political accountability in play: the Budd Inquiry and David Blunkett's resignation. *Public Law,* 229–38.

Brazier, R. (1994) It is a constitutional issue: fitness for ministerial office in the 1990s. *Public Law,* 431–51.

Editorial (2007) Losing heads over the lost data. *Justice of the Peace,* 171: 841.

Hadfield, B. (2005) Devolution, Westminster and the English question. *Public Law,* 286–305.

Khushal Murkens, J.E. (2017) A special section on R (Miller) v Secretary of State for Exiting the European Union, Mixed Messages in Bottles: the European Union, Devolution, and the Future of the Constitution. *Modern Law Review,* 80(4): 685.

Longley, D. and Lewis, N. (1996) Ministerial responsibility: the next steps. *Public Law,* 490–507.

Poole, T. (2017) Devotion to legalism: on the Brexit case. *Modern Law Review,* 80(4): 696.

Reid, C. (2003) The limits of devolved legislative power: subordinate legislation in Scotland. *Statute Law Review,* 24: 187–210.

Reid, C. (2017) Opinion: Brexit and the devolution dynamics. *Environmental Law Review,* 19(1): 3–5.

Scott, R. (1996) Ministerial accountability. *Public Law,* 410–26.

Steyn, Lord (2006) Democracy, the rule of law and the role of judges. *European Human Rights Law Review,* 3: 243–53.

Trench, A. (2006) The Government of Wales Act 2006: the next steps on devolution for Wales. *Public Law,* 687–96.

www.pearsoned.co.uk/lawexpress

Go online to access more revision support including quizzes to test your knowledge, sample questions with answer guidelines, printable versions of the topic maps, and more!

Institutions of state 2

5

Revision checklist

Essential points you should know:

☐ The composition and structure of the legislature

☐ The legislative function of Parliament

☐ The passage of primary and secondary legislation and the relationship between the two forms of provision

☐ The scrutiny function of Parliament and the effectiveness of the various mechanisms for scrutiny

☐ The nature and scope of parliamentary privilege

Topic map

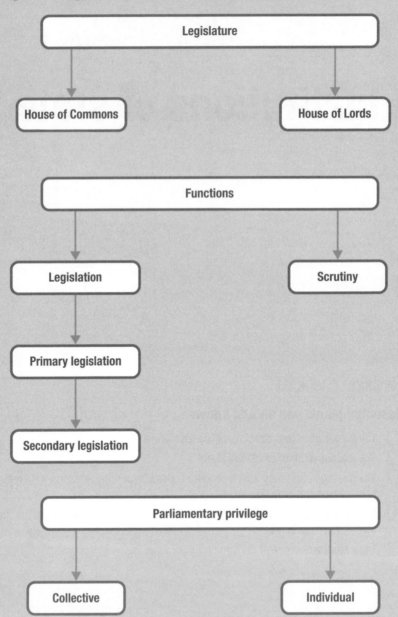

A printable version of this topic map is available from www.pearsoned.co.uk/lawexpress

■ Introduction

Of all the institutions of state, Parliament has the most important functions to perform.

The previous chapter considered the role of the monarch, judiciary and executive within the constitution. This chapter examines the work of the final institution of state: the legislature (Parliament). Remember, under the doctrine of parliamentary sovereignty outlined in Chapter 3, Parliament is the most powerful of the institutions of state. Therefore, you must be able to discuss the work of Parliament and consider its contribution to the operation of the state.

ASSESSMENT ADVICE

Essay questions

Essay questions on the scrutiny function of Parliament are quite common. The important point to remember about such questions is that the examiner will not just want a list of the various mechanisms for scrutiny, but will also want to see some assessment of their effectiveness. It is this analytical element to your answer which will gain the higher marks.

Problem questions

Problem questions on Parliament usually centre on the operation of parliamentary privilege, and often require you to differentiate between the absolute privilege enjoyed by MPs and the qualified privilege enjoyed by the media. Here examiners will want to see a clear understanding of the differences between the two forms of privilege and also the ability to apply the rules to the facts of the scenario.

■ Sample question

Could you answer this question? Below is a typical essay question that could arise on this topic. Guidelines on answering the question are included at the end of this chapter, whilst a sample problem question and guidance on tackling it can be found on the companion website.

ESSAY QUESTION

One of the key functions of Parliament is to scrutinise the operation of the executive. Assess how effective the existing parliamentary mechanisms for scrutiny are in achieving this objective.

📖 **REVISION NOTE**

Remember that any consideration of the role of Parliament must acknowledge the doctrine of parliamentary sovereignty. Therefore, when discussing the functions of Parliament, it is important to emphasise that it is because it is sovereign that it is Parliament (rather than any of the other institutions of state) which creates statute and scrutinises the work of the executive.

❗ Don't be tempted to . . .

Parliament and executive

One of the most common mistakes made by students in exams is to confuse the terms 'legislature' and 'executive'. Always be clear that the legislature is Parliament (comprising over 600 MPs), whereas the executive is the government or the Cabinet of ministers.

Also, it can be confusing to have to jump between the terms 'legislature' and 'Parliament', depending on the discussion. Discussions on the separation of powers speak of 'the legislature', whereas answers on parliamentary sovereignty speak of 'Parliament'. Don't worry too much about which term you use as long as you do not confuse it with the executive.

■ The legislature

The UK has a 'bicameral legislature' (i.e. composed of two chambers). These are the House of Commons and the House of Lords.

The House of Commons

The House of Commons is the dominant chamber, as it is elected and so has a democratic mandate. The party with the most seats in the House of Commons forms the government.

Total number of MPs	650
(As at October 2017):	
Conservative	316
Scottish National Party	35
Liberal Democrat ('Lib Dem')	12
Labour	262
Others	24
Government majority at last election	0

Make your answer stand out

In answering any question on Parliament, make clear that the current government does not actually hold the majority of seats in the House of Commons and so has been forced to form a so-called 'minority government' with the support of the Democratic Unionist Party (DUP). This makes the government very vulnerable to rebellion by its own backbenchers, i.e. if only one or two Conservative MPS refuse to support the government in a vote, it could lose.

Aside from the outcome, the 2017 general election was also notable as it represented the first election called following a motion 'that there shall be an early election under s. 2(1)–(4) of the Fixed-term Parliaments Act 2011 – the Act which was meant to ensure that general elections were held every five years.

It is also important to recognise that the current state of the parties in the House of Commons is the result of the 'first past the post' election system, which is widely criticised for not being truly representative of votes cast. As an example, the UK Independence Party (UKIP) secured over three million votes in the 2015 general election, but this produced only one MP in Parliament. It has been estimated that, under a system of proportional representation (PR), the party could have taken over 80 seats with the same number of votes. Successive governments have resisted introducing a system of proportional representation, as it would reduce their majority and force them to work more closely with their opponents, but many argue that a proportional system would be fairer. For discussion of the issues, see the report of the Jenkins Commission (1998).

The House of Lords

The House of Lords is known as the 'second chamber' and is not elected, being largely appointed. It is often referred to as a 'revising chamber', there to advise the Commons and serve as a 'voice of reason'.

Total number of Lords (as at October 2017)	799
Labour	199
Conservative	252
Lib Dem	100
Crossbench	180
Others	44
Bishops	24

Make your answer stand out

Reform of the House of Lords is a topical issue and examiners will give credit for an understanding of the difficulties faced by the government in trying to modernise the upper House, particularly as there seems to be little agreement on the best way forward. For an overview of the discussion, see Phillipson (2004). You might also comment on the referendum held in Ireland to abolish their upper chamber (the Seanad) in October 2013. The public voted to retain the second house of the legislature, but on the basis of a very low voter turnout.

Functions of Parliament

There are two key functions of Parliament: legislation and scrutiny.

Legislation

Parliament approves between 60 and 70 Bills per year, creating Acts of Parliament. There are various types of Bill:

Public Bill	Affects everyone
Private Bill	Applies to specific people or organisations
Private Member's Bill	Introduced by an MP who is not a member of the government

Legislative process

First reading	The title of the Bill is read out in the House of Commons.
Second reading	The responsible minister sets out the purpose of the Bill to Parliament, and the opposition responds. There is then a debate in the House.
Committee stage	The Bill is referred to a committee (usually a Public Bill Committee), which considers the Bill line by line and which may make amendments.
Report stage	The Bill is reported back to the House, which may accept or reject any amendments.
Third reading	This is largely a formality to correct any errors.
The Lords	The Bill is sent to the Lords. The above process is repeated in the Lords.
Royal assent	Announced in the Commons and the Lords.

KEY STATUTE

Parliament Act 1911, section 2(1)

If any Public Bill (other than a Money Bill or a Bill containing any provision to extend the maximum duration of Parliament beyond five years) is passed by the House of Commons [in two successive sessions] (whether of the same Parliament or not), and . . . is rejected by the House of Lords in each of those sessions, that Bill shall, on its rejection [for the second time] by the House of Lords, unless the House of Commons direct to the contrary, be presented to His Majesty and become an Act of Parliament on the Royal Assent being signified thereto, notwithstanding that the House of Lords have not consented to the Bill.

 Make your answer stand out

Any examination answer which mentions the Parliament Act 1911 will benefit from a careful reading of the comments of Lord Bingham in *Jackson and others* v *Attorney General* [2005] UKHL 56 (HL).

Primary and secondary legislation

It is important to differentiate between primary and secondary legislation.

Primary legislation

Primary legislation consists of the Acts of Parliament, discussed above.

Secondary legislation

Sometimes, an Act of Parliament (known as the 'parent Act') will give the power to make rules/regulations/codes of practice to a minister, local authority or other department. Such rules/regulations/codes of practice are '**secondary legislation**' (also known as 'delegated legislation' or 'subordinate legislation') and are used to save parliamentary time. The crucial differences between primary and secondary legislation are:

- Primary legislation is debated by Parliament. Secondary legislation is not.
- Primary legislation cannot be challenged by the courts. The operation of secondary legislation can be challenged by means of judicial review.

Make your answer stand out

Note that one of the most contentious aspects of the government's 'Great Repeal Bill' is the facility under so-called 'Henry VIII' clauses for the government to amend legislation without full parliamentary debate

□ REVISION NOTE

The distinction between primary and secondary legislation is particularly important in relation to judicial review and the power of the courts to challenge the use of powers granted under secondary legislation. Do not make the mistake of suggesting that an Act of Parliament may be challenged by means of judicial review.

KEY STATUTE

Police and Criminal Evidence Act 1984, section 66

The Secretary of State shall issue codes of practice in connection with –

(a) the exercise by police officers of statutory powers –

    (i) to search a person without first arresting him; or

    (ii) to search a vehicle without making an arrest;

(b) the detention, treatment, questioning and identification of persons by police officers;

(c) searches of premises by police officers; and

(d) the seizure of property found by police officers on persons or premises.

Scrutiny

Parliament also scrutinises the work of the executive to ensure the government is functioning effectively and not abusing its powers. This is achieved by a number of mechanisms:

Mechanism	Format	Advantages	Disadvantages
Prime Minister's Questions (PMQs)	30 minutes' questions once a week	Puts the PM on the spot before Parliament	Theatrical, often has little substance
Ministerial questions	Each minister must answer questions once every 3–4 weeks	Ministers are held to account and must provide information	Dull and poorly attended

Mechanism	Format	Advantages	Disadvantages
Debates	Varies depending on type of debate	Forces government to justify its actions	Often very short and limited in number
Select committees	Each Ministry has a committee to oversee its work. The committee can demand papers and call witnesses	Thorough and ongoing scrutiny of the government	Only advisory – have no powers to impose sanctions

> ✎ EXAM TIP
>
> In considering Parliament's scrutiny of the executive, always emphasise that some mechanisms (such as Prime Minister's Questions) are widely perceived as ineffective as methods of holding the government to account compared with others (such as select committees). This must be balanced, however, against the other supposed benefits of PMQs, such as providing the Prime Minister and the leader of the opposition with an opportunity to raise the morale of their parties by means of a confident performance.

> ❗ Don't be tempted to . . .
>
> ## Committees
>
> Be careful not to confuse *select* committees with the committees which consider new legislative proposals during the 'committee stage'. **Select committees** examine the work of a particular government department.

Parliamentary privilege

One important aspect of Parliament which frequently features in examinations relates to the privileges which Parliament enjoys. **Parliamentary privileges** can be categorised as 'collective' and 'individual' privileges.

Collective privilege

These are the privileges which attach to Parliament as an institution and relate to matters such as admissions, expulsions and disciplinary matters. It is important to remember that Parliament makes its own rules and procedures, in much the same way as a club or society.

KEY CASE

Bradlaugh v *Gossett* (1884) 12 QBD 271 (DC)

Concerning: admission to take up a seat in Parliament

Facts

B had been elected but was an atheist and so would not swear the parliamentary oath to God, so the House of Commons refused to allow him to take his seat.

Legal principle

The court held that the jurisdiction of the House of Commons over its members was absolute – there was nothing the court could do. Lord Coleridge CJ: 'What is said or done within the walls of Parliament cannot be inquired into in a court of law . . . '

KEY CASE

R v *Graham-Campbell and others, ex parte Herbert* [1935] 1 KB 594 (DC)

Concerning: the sale of alcohol without a licence in Parliament

Facts

Alcohol was sold within the House of Commons despite the fact that Parliament did not have a licence as required by law.

Legal principle

The court held that this fell within the privileges of the House. Avory J: 'No court of law has jurisdiction to entertain such an application as was made in this case.'

Privilege and contempt

Any breach of privilege (i.e. breach of the rules of Parliament) amounts to contempt, which can lead to Parliament imposing a punishment on MPs. Contempt of Parliament includes:

- disorderly conduct;
- misleading the House;
- bribery and corruption;
- refusing to cooperate with a Parliamentary committee.

Punishments

Censure	MP receives a reprimand from the Speaker
Suspension	An MP can be suspended for contempt for a period from one day to the entire parliamentary session
Imprisonment	MPs can be imprisoned in Big Ben, outsiders taken to a prison (not used since 1880)
Expulsion	The most serious punishment is for an MP to be expelled from the House

Individual privilege

As well as the collective privileges which attach to Parliament as an institution, there are also privileges which are enjoyed by MPs as individuals.

Freedom from arrest

MPs have freedom from arrest, but this only applies to civil arrest, not an arrest relating to criminal offences. Therefore, this only really applies to arrest for contempt of court (e.g. non-payment of damages in a civil case), and so is not a meaningful protection for MPs.

> **✎ EXAM TIP**
>
> When discussing freedom from arrest, make sure to point out that the immunity from arrest applies from 40 days before the parliamentary session begins to 40 days after the session ends. It is also worth noting that the privilege had far greater importance in the days of the debtor's prison, when a person could be imprisoned for non-payment of a debt.

Freedom of speech

Of far greater significance is the freedom of speech which is enjoyed by MPs. This means that an MP is immune from suit for defamation (libel or slander) for anything said as part of 'proceedings in Parliament'. This is justified on the grounds that it allows Parliament to function more efficiently by permitting MPs to speak freely, without fear of legal action.

KEY CASE

Dillon v *Balfour* (1887) 20 LR Ir 600 (Ct TBC)

Concerning: parliamentary privilege and freedom of speech

Facts

A minister made a statement in Parliament that a midwife had deliberately refused to attend to a pregnant woman. The midwife attempted to sue for slander.

Legal principle

The court refused to hear the action as the statement was covered by parliamentary privilege.

'Proceedings in Parliament'

The privilege enjoyed by MPs is absolute (i.e. it does not matter if the statement was deliberate and malicious), but applies only to 'proceedings in Parliament'. This clearly applies to speeches within Parliament, during debates, etc., but the position is less clear with communications which move outside the buildings themselves (e.g. letters).

KEY CASE

Rivlin v *Bilainkin* [1953] 1 QB 485 (QBD)

Concerning: the meaning of 'proceedings in Parliament'

Facts

The claimant in an action for defamation had obtained an injunction preventing the defendant from repeating the 'defamatory' statement. The defendant repeated the statement in a letter and delivered copies to a number of MPs. The letters were posted in the House of Commons post office, within the House of Commons.

Legal principle

It was held that, as the allegations were purely personal in nature and did not concern the business of the House, they could not be 'proceedings in Parliament' and, therefore, were not covered by privilege. McNair, J: 'I am satisfied that no question of privilege arises, for a variety of reasons, and particularly I rely on the fact that the publication was not connected in any way with any proceedings in that House.'

The 'Strauss case' HC 227 [1957–58], HC Deb, vol 591, col 208 (8 July)

Concerning: the meaning of 'proceedings in Parliament'

Facts

George Strauss MP wrote to a minister complaining about the activities of the London Electricity Board. The minister passed the letter to the Board, who threatened to sue Strauss for libel.

Principle

The House of Commons Committee for Privileges held that this fell within 'proceedings in Parliament' and was, therefore, privileged, but a vote within the House of Commons rejected this and held that it was not 'proceedings in Parliament' and so did not attract privilege.

It seems, therefore, that 'proceedings in Parliament' is limited to statements and communications directly concerned with the business of Parliament, either conducted within the Chamber or, in the case of letters, etc., directly related to ongoing parliamentary business.

Reporting of statements made in Parliament

Although MPs enjoy **absolute privilege** in relation to statements made in Parliament, the position is different when those statements are reported by others. Here, the privilege may be absolute or qualified, depending on who reports the statement.

Parliamentary Papers Act 1840

The Act confers absolute privilege on papers either produced by the House (e.g. *Hansard*) or authorised by the House.

Statements by third parties

The position is different again for newspapers and other publications which publish what has been said in Parliament. They cannot claim absolute privilege and can only claim the common law defence of **qualified privilege**, which requires the statement to be fair, accurate and without malice.

There is also a defence of qualified privilege under the Defamation Act 1996.

KEY STATUTE

Defamation Act 1996, section 15(1) and Schedule 1, Paragraph 1

Section 15(1) The publication of any report or other statement mentioned in Schedule 1 to this Act is privileged unless the publication is shown to be made with malice.

Schedule 1, Paragraph 1

A fair and accurate report of proceedings in public of a legislature anywhere in the world.

KEY CASE

Makudi v *Baron Triesman of Tottenham* [2014] All ER (D) 242 (CA)

Concerning: parliamentary privilege

Facts

Lord Triesman, who had been Chairman of the English Football Association (FA), gave evidence to the Culture, Media and Sport Committee of the House of Commons. As part of his evidence he made comments about the claimant, which prompted a claim for defamation and malicious falsehood. Shortly afterwards, the FA appointed a QC to conduct a review of the allegations and Lord Triesman was interviewed and repeated his comments. What had been said before the parliamentary committee was clearly covered by Article 9 of the Bill of Rights 1689 which provides '[t]hat the freedom of speech, and debates or proceedings in Parliament, ought not to be impeached or questioned in any court or place outside of Parliament'. The question for the court was whether this parliamentary privilege extended to the later interview.

Legal principle

Held: The protection of Article 9 can extend to extra-Parliamentary speech. Laws LJ: 'Generally I think such cases will possess these two characteristics: (1) a public interest in repetition of the Parliamentary utterance which the speaker ought reasonably to serve, and (2) so close a nexus between the occasions of his speaking, in and then out of Parliament, that the prospect of his obligation to speak on the second occasion (or the expectation or promise that he would do so) is reasonably foreseeable at the time of the first and his purpose in speaking on both occasions is the same or very closely related . . . Looking at the case in the round, in my judgment [the statement in this case] possesses both of the characteristics.'

■ Putting it all together

Answer guidelines

See the essay question at the start of the chapter.

Approaching the question

- Adopt a methodical approach to the topic, stating clearly the role of parliamentary scrutiny before considering the various mechanisms in turn.
- List the key features of each mechanism and indicate their main advantages and disadvantages.
- Remember to write a fully formed conclusion which offers some reflection on the question and some evaluation of the most and least effective mechanism for scrutiny.

Important points to include

- The question does not just require you to list the mechanisms for scrutiny, but also to assess their effectiveness.
- Explain the requirement for the executive to be accountable to Parliament as the elected representatives of the people.
- Always remember to offer some conclusion as to how well the system of scrutiny operates (e.g. pointing out the effectiveness of mechanisms such as select committees compared to others such as Prime Minister's Questions).

✓ Make your answer stand out

- Remember to relate the concept of parliamentary scrutiny to the doctrine of parliamentary sovereignty. Explain why it is inevitable that it should be Parliament, rather than any other institution of state, which scrutinises the work of the executive.
- Rather than merely listing the mechanisms, give some brief explanation of how they operate.
- In relation to Prime Minister's Questions, emphasise that the event is as much for party morale (to see the leader perform well in Parliament) as for real scrutiny.
- In the current climate of a coalition government and hung Parliament, it is worth questioning whether scrutiny is as effective as it might be when there is single party government.

READ TO IMPRESS

Blackburn, R. (2011) The 2010 general election outcome and formation of the Conservative–Liberal Democrat coalition government. *Public Law,* 30–55.

Feldman, D. (2004) The impact of human rights on the UK legislative process. *Statute Law Review,* 25: 91.

Hazell, R. (2006) Time for a new convention: parliamentary scrutiny of constitutional bills 1997–2005. *Public Law,* 247–98.

Lester, A. (2002) Parliamentary scrutiny of legislation under the Human Rights Act 1998. *European Human Rights Law Review,* 4: 432–51.

McHarg, A. (2006) What is delegated legislation? *Public Law,* 539–61.

McKeown, M. and Thomson, S. (2010) The role of the House of Lords in a hung parliament. *Statute Law Review,* 19: 99–103.

Oliver, D. (2006) Improving the scrutiny of bills: the case for standards and checklists. *Public Law,* 219–46.

Parpworth, N. (2017) Plus ça change? *New Law Journal,* 7747: 14.

Phillipson, G. (2004) 'The greatest quango of them all', 'a rival chamber' or 'hybrid non-sense': solving the second chamber paradox. *Public Law,* 352–79.

Report of the Independent Commission on the Voting System (Jenkins Commission Report) (1998). London: HMSO. Available online at http://researchbriefings.files.parliament.uk/documents/RP98-112/RP98-112.pdf.

Squires, D. (2000) Challenging subordinate legislation under the Human Rights Act. *European Human Rights Law Review,* 2: 116–30.

www.pearsoned.co.uk/lawexpress

Go online to access more revision support including quizzes to test your knowledge, sample questions with answer guidelines, printable versions of the topic maps, and more!

Civil liberties and human rights

6

Revision checklist

Essential points you should know:

☐ The traditionally precarious status of civil liberties in the UK as residual 'freedoms' rather than positive 'rights'

☐ The impact of the European Convention on Human Rights and how cases were brought before the European Court of Human Rights from the UK

☐ The impact of the Human Rights Act 1998

☐ The constitutional implications of the 1998 Act and the relationship between Parliament and the courts

☐ Current protections for human rights in the UK

■ Topic map

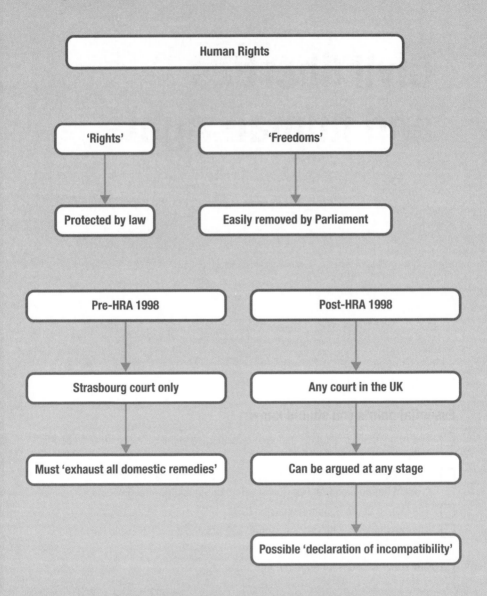

A printable version of this topic map is available from www.pearsoned.co.uk/lawexpress

■ Introduction

Increased protection for human rights is the most important development in UK law for generations.

Although the Human Rights Act 1998 is now well established, it is important to recognise that it was a huge step for the legal system and the constitution. Consequently, examiners will almost certainly make some reference to the Act in exams, either as a 'stand-alone' topic or as part of a question on another subject. Therefore, the ability to discuss the Act and its implications will always help you to gain a higher mark.

ASSESSMENT ADVICE

Essay questions

Essay questions on human rights in the UK and, in particular, the implications of the Human Rights Act (HRA) 1998 are very common. Such questions require you to chart the development of human rights protection, and it is possible to score highly provided you are clear on the main stages in the process and on the way in which HRA 1998 has increased the accessibility of the rights under the European Convention on Human Rights (the Convention/ECHR) for the individual. Post-Brexit referendum, it is also possible that you will be asked to consider the longstanding Conservative proposal to replace the ECHR rights with a British 'Bill of Rights'. However, as with the rest of the Brexit debate, there is much uncertainty as to the likely outcome. Whatever the question, always remember to include plenty of examples to support the points you are making.

Problem questions

Problem questions are less common, but you may face a scenario based around an individual who wishes to enforce their rights before the courts. Here it is essential to have some knowledge of the individual Convention rights, together with an understanding of the procedure under the Human Rights Act 1998.

■ Sample question

Could you answer this question? Below is a typical essay question that could arise on this topic. Guidelines on answering the question are included at the end of this chapter, whilst a sample problem question and guidance on tackling it can be found on the companion website.

ESSAY QUESTION

Assess the impact of the Human Rights Act 1998 on the protection of individual rights in the UK.

▉ Human rights in the UK

KEY DEFINITION: RIGHTS

There is no single definition of the term 'rights', but a number of legal theorists have suggested possible meanings of the word. One of the most commonly cited definitions comes from Wesley Hohfeld who divided rights into 'privileges', 'claims', 'powers' and 'immunities'. The sorts of civil liberties which we normally think of when discussing rights would fall into Hohfeld's definition of a 'claim' right – we have a claim against the state to uphold our 'rights'.

There are three stages involved in considering the development of human rights protection in the UK: the traditional 'freedoms' model under the unwritten constitution, the position under the European Convention on Human Rights and, finally, the current position following implementation of the Human Rights Act 1998. Any exam question on human rights in the UK will require you to describe these stages.

▉ The traditional 'freedoms' model

If we think of a 'right' as something which we are able to do and which the state cannot take away, then the unwritten constitution of the UK has traditionally provided little protection for such **rights**.

□ REVISION NOTE

The topic of rights should be revised alongside Chapter 1 on the nature of the constitution and also the section in Chapter 3 on parliamentary sovereignty, since both topics play an important part in an understanding of the traditional approach to rights in the UK.

Remember that one of the key differences between the unwritten constitution of the UK and the written constitutions of most other countries is that written constitutions contain a number of fundamental rights (such as the right to bear arms in the USA). Also, the written constitution is a 'higher' source of law, which cannot be easily changed by the government. This means that such rights cannot ordinarily be taken away by the government.

In the UK the position has been very different. Here, there is no written constitution to form a 'higher' source of law and the doctrine of parliamentary sovereignty provides that there is no area where Parliament cannot legislate. This has meant that any so-called 'right' could be taken away by an Act of Parliament.

KEY STATUTE

Firearms (Amendment) Act 1997

Prior to the Dunblane school massacre in 1996, members of gun clubs had been allowed to keep properly registered guns. In the aftermath of the shooting, the government banned most handguns, thereby removing what gun owners saw as their 'right' to own guns.

KEY STATUTE

Hunting Act 2004, section 1

A person commits an offence if he hunts a wild mammal with a dog, unless his hunting is exempt.

Despite vigorous lobbying from those involved in hunting, the 2004 Act removed what hunters assumed to be their 'right' to hunt.

In this way, rather than having 'rights', citizens in the UK have enjoyed the 'freedom' to do anything which the state has not defined as illegal – which is not the same thing!

! Don't be tempted to . . .

'Rights' vs 'freedoms'

The distinction between 'rights' and 'freedoms' is an important one and so it is crucial that you do not confuse these concepts. Examiners will credit an understanding of the distinction between the two and the different legal implications of each. In this way, be sure to emphasise the difference between a 'right', which can be claimed, and a 'freedom', which exists only until the state removes it. The above examples on changes to the law relating to handgun ownership and hunting with hounds are useful examples to cite in support of this point.

Make your answer stand out

The examiner will always be impressed by students who can make links between the various topics, rather than treating them as entirely separate. Therefore, in discussing the vulnerability of rights under the unwritten constitution of the UK, you should emphasise ▶

that this is consistent with Dicey's model of parliamentary sovereignty discussed in Chapter 3. In particular, it would contradict the principle that Parliament can legislate on any area if a particular right was enshrined and so could not be taken away by legislation.

■ The European Convention on Human Rights

Signed in 1950 in response to the injustices of the Second World War, the Articles of the Convention contain a number of fundamental human rights:

Article 1 – Obligation on Signatories to Respect Human Rights

Article 2 – the Right to Life

Article 3 – the Prohibition on Torture

Article 4 – the Prohibition on Slavery

Article 5 – the Right to Liberty and Security

Article 6 – the Right to a Fair Trial

Article 7 – the Right not to be Punished Except for Breach of the Law

Article 8 – the Right to Respect for Private Life

Article 9 – the Right to Freedom of Conscience, Thought and Religion

Article 10 – the Right to Freedom of Expression

Article 11 – the Right to Freedom of Assembly and Association

Article 12 – the Right to Marry

Article 13 – the Right to an Effective Remedy

Article 14 – the Prohibition on Discrimination (in relation to the Convention Rights)

Cases alleging breaches of Convention rights are heard by the European Court of Human Rights in Strasbourg.

✎ EXAM TIP

When discussing human rights cases, always be careful not to become confused with EU law in general. For example, human rights cases are heard by the European Court of Human Rights (ECtHR), not by the European Court of Justice (ECJ).

■ The European Convention and the UK

The European Convention was not incorporated into UK law until the passage of the Human Rights Act 1998. However, that is not to say that the Convention did not affect the law and the

THE EUROPEAN CONVENTION AND THE UK

people of the UK. As signatories to the Convention, the UK government was bound to its terms as a matter of international law, but, crucially, this did not confer rights on individual citizens.

> **❗ Don't be tempted to . . .**
>
> ## The Convention and the UK
>
> Understanding the relationship between the Convention and UK law before the 1998 Act came into force can be confusing. The principal point to remember is that, in order to uphold their Convention rights, UK citizens had to take a case to the Strasbourg Court and they could not do this until they had 'exhausted all domestic remedies' – i.e. been through the entire UK legal system, up to and including the House of Lords (now replaced by the Supreme Court).

Where the UK was found to have breached Convention rights, the government usually changed the law to remove the inconsistency. This can be seen in the following examples.

KEY CASE

Malone v *Metropolitan Police Commissioner (No. 2)* [1979] Ch 344 (CH)

Concerning: alleged breach of Article 8 (Right to Respect for Private Life)

Facts

The plaintiff argued that his telephone had been bugged by the police without lawful authority, thereby breaching his right to privacy.

Legal principle

The court refused to recognise that such a right existed in English law and held that no such right could be imported from Article 8 of the Convention. Megarry VC: 'it can lawfully be done simply because there is nothing to make it unlawful'.

KEY CASE

Malone v *United Kingdom* (1984) 7 EHRR 14 (ECtHR)

Concerning: alleged breach of Article 8 (Right to Respect for Private Life)

Facts

Malone took his case to the European Court of Human Rights and argued the facts as above.

▶

95

Legal principle

The ECtHR held that the telephone-tapping powers in the UK did contravene Article 8, as they were not subject to clear and accountable legal procedures. Judge Wiarda: 'the minimum degree of legal protection to which citizens are entitled under the rule of law in a democratic society is lacking'.

As a result, the UK Parliament passed the Interception of Communications Act 1985 to provide statutory authority for telephone tapping.

KEY STATUTE

Interception of Communications Act 1985, section 1(1), (2)

(1) Subject to the following provisions of this section, a person who intentionally intercepts a communication in the course of its transmission by post or by means of a public telecommunication system shall be guilty of an offence and liable

(a) on summary conviction, to a fine not exceeding the statutory maximum;
(b) on conviction on indictment, to imprisonment for a term not exceeding two years or to a fine or to both.

(2) A person shall not be guilty of an offence under this section if –

(a) the communication is intercepted in obedience to a warrant issued by the Secretary of State under section 2 below; or
(b) that person has reasonable grounds for believing that the person to whom, or the person by whom, the communication is sent has consented to the interception.

 Make your answer stand out

Point out that the delay and expense of going through the entire legal system before being able to take a case to Strasbourg meant that many potentially valid cases fell by the wayside, which was beneficial to the government as the defendant in each case.

■ The Human Rights Act 1998

The 1998 Act made the Convention rights directly enforceable in the domestic courts. This means that, instead of having to go to the Strasbourg Court, a person can argue breaches of their rights under the Convention in any court in the UK. However, one important limitation is that the Convention rights are only 'vertically directly effective' (i.e. they can only be enforced against the state) and not 'horizontally directly effective' (enforceable against other individuals). The Act defines this in terms of 'public authorities'.

KEY STATUTE

Human Rights Act 1998, section 6(1)

It is unlawful for a public authority to act in a way which is incompatible with a Convention right.

The role of the courts

One of the most important aspects of the Human Rights Act 1998 is the role of the courts in upholding the Convention rights. This has two key elements: first, as has already been noted, the 1998 Act allows claimants to argue breach of their Convention rights in the domestic courts, so judges in any court in the UK may be faced with issues of human rights which were previously reserved for the Strasbourg Court; second, when faced with such a claim, the courts must decide whether the UK law is consistent with or breaches the Convention right. This is a significant development of the court's role.

KEY STATUTE

Human Rights Act 1998, section 3(1)

So far as it is possible to do so, primary legislation and subordinate legislation must be read and given effect in a way which is compatible with the Convention rights.

Under this section, the court must interpret the UK statute in a way which is compatible with the Convention rights if it is possible to do so. Of course, the wording of the provision acknowledges that there may be occasions where it is impossible for the court to interpret the domestic statute in a way which is compatible with the Convention.

 Make your answer stand out

The requirement imposed on the courts by section 3 is a marked departure from the traditional rules of statutory interpretation, and sees the court potentially ignoring what Parliament intended in order to reconcile the domestic statute with the Convention right. For further discussion, see Kavanagh (2006).

> **! Don't be tempted to . . .**
>
> **The duty under HRA 1998**
>
> Don't fall into the trap of saying that the courts must interpret UK statutes in a way which is compatible with the Convention rights. The inclusion of the phrase 'So far as it is possible to do so' leaves open the possibility that a statute can be held to be incompatible.

Declarations of incompatibility

As has already been noted, although section 3 requires the court to interpret statutes in a way which is compatible with the Convention, there may be situations where the wording of the statute is so clear and unambiguous that it cannot be interpreted in any way other than in conflict with a Convention right. In such cases the court must make a 'declaration of incompatibility' (i.e. that the domestic statute is incompatible with the Convention).

KEY CASE

R (on the application of H) v London North and East Region Mental Health Review Tribunal **[2002] QB 1 (CA)**

Concerning: compatibility of domestic law with European Convention on Human Rights

Facts

H was detained in a mental hospital under the Mental Health Act 1983. He applied to the tribunal to be released, but this required him to prove to the tribunal that the conditions for detention no longer applied. When his application was refused, H sought judicial review of the decision.

Legal principle

It was held that the requirement on H to prove that detention was no longer required imposed on him a reverse burden of proof which was incompatible with Article 5. Therefore, a declaration of incompatibility would be made. Lord Phillips MR: 'We have concluded that [the provisions of the Act] are incompatible with both Article 5(1) and Article 5(4)).'

KEY CASE

Wilson v First County Trust Ltd **[2002] QB 74 (CA)**

Concerning: compatibility of domestic law with European Convention on Human Rights

Facts

A loan agreement between the claimant and defendant pawnbrokers failed to correctly state the amount of credit. Section 127(3) of the Consumer Credit Act 1974 barred the court from enforcing the agreement.

Legal principle

The court held that the absolute bar on enforcement was an infringement of the right to a fair trial and the right to protection of property guaranteed by Article 6(1) of the European Convention. Sir Andrew Morritt VC: 'The question, therefore, is whether, as a matter of discretion, a declaration of incompatibility should be made in the present case. In our view it is right to do so.'

KEY CASE

R (on the application of Wright) v *Secretary of State for Health* [2009] UKHL 1 (HL)

Concerning: compatibility of domestic law with European Convention on Human Rights

Facts

Under the Care Standards Act 2000, care workers employed to look after vulnerable adults could be placed on a list of people considered unsuitable to undertake such work. The effect of listing was to deprive them of their employment as a care worker and to prevent them from gaining other such employment. The Act provided for a judicial hearing only after a lengthy administrative process during most of which the worker was provisionally on the list. The claimants argued that the scheme was incompatible with their rights under Articles 6 and 8.

Legal principle

In upholding the original decision (and overturning the decision of the Court of Appeal), the House of Lords held that the procedure for provisional listing did not meet the requirements of Article 6(1). The 2000 Act was accordingly incompatible with the Convention. Baroness Hale: 'No other solution could properly be adopted by way of the interpretative obligation in section 3(1) of the Human Rights Act 1998.'

KEY CASE

R (F) (a child) v *Secretary of State for the Home Department* [2010] UKSC 17 (SC)

Concerning: declaration of incompatibility

Facts

Section 82 of the Sexual Offences Act 2003 required anyone sentenced to 30 months' imprisonment or more for a sexual offence to notify the police of where they were living ▶

and of any travel abroad. This duty applied for the rest of their lives and there was no right to seek a review of the notification requirements. The claimant argued that the absence of any right to a review rendered the notification requirements incompatible with the right to respect for his private and family life under Article 8 of the ECHR.

Legal principle

It was held that, in the case of a person on the sex offender register who was able to demonstrate that they no longer posed a risk, there was no justification for continued interference with their Article 8 rights by insisting on future compliance with reporting requirements. Therefore, the court affirmed a declaration of incompatibility to the effect that the absence of any mechanism for review of the requirements under the 2003 Act was a disproportionate interference with the rights under Article 8.

KEY CASE

Benkharbouche and another v Embassy of the Republic of Sudan (Secretary of State for Foreign and Commonwealth Affairs and others intervening) **[2015] EWCA Civ 33 (CA)**

Concerning: declaration of incompatibility

Facts

A Moroccan national was employed as a cook at the Sudanese embassy in London. She was dismissed and brought claims for unfair dismissal, failure to pay the minimum wage and breach of the Working Time Regulations 1998. Another Moroccan national was employed as a member of the domestic staff of the Libyan embassy in London. She was dismissed and brought claims for unfair dismissal, arrears of pay, racial discrimination and harassment, and breach of the Working Time Regulations 1998. Both Sudan and Libya claimed state immunity under section 1 of the State Immunity Act 1978 (SIA). The issues in the appeal were (a) whether the claims engaged Article 6 ECHR, and (b) if so, whether the provisions of the 1978 Act could be interpreted in a manner consistent with Article 6.

Legal principle

Held: the relevant provisions of the 1978 Act infringed Article 6 ECHR and could not be read down and given effect in a way which is compatible with ECHR under the interpretative obligation imposed by HRA 1998. Reading down means choosing a compatible interpretation where more than one interpretation is strictly possible. As a consequence, the court would make a declaration of incompatibility pursuant to section 4(2) HRA 1998. Lord Dyson MR: 'We conclude that a rule of the breadth of section 16(1)(a) SIA is not required by international law and is not within the range of tenable views of what is required by international law. Accordingly, in its application to the claims of these claimants, section 16(1)(a) SIA is incompatible with Article 6 ECHR.'

Make your answer stand out

For an example of how the courts approach questions of compatibility with Convention rights, see the recent decision of the Supreme Court in *Lawrence and another* v *Fen Tigers Ltd and others (No. 3) (Secretary of State for Justice and others intervening)* [2015] 1 WLR 3485.

If the court makes a declaration of incompatibility, it is open to Parliament to change the statute in order to remove the conflict with the Convention rights. For example, as a result of the decision in *R(F)* above, a review procedure for the indefinite notice requirements under the 2003 Act was introduced. Note that Parliament can also refuse to remedy the incompatibility, but there will be considerable political pressure on it to do so, not least because those adversely affected by the failure to uphold their Convention rights may be able to sue the state for damages. It should also be noted that a large proportion of such declarations are overturned on appeal.

✎ **EXAM TIP**

In discussing declarations of incompatibility, you can mention *R (Black)* v *Secretary of State for Justice* [2009] UKHL 1 and *Nasseri* v *Secretary of State for the Home Department* [2009] UKHL 23 as examples of declarations subsequently being overturned on appeal.

 Make your answer stand out

Remember that the final decision as to whether to alter the statute in question lies with Parliament – thereby retaining parliamentary sovereignty. The government had to include this in the Human Rights Bill in order for Parliament to approve it. Examiners will give you credit for recognising that Parliament still retains the ultimate power in such circumstances.

The future of HRA 1998

There have been enduring calls for the repeal of HRA 1998 in favour of a 'British Bill of Rights', particularly from the right wing Conservative Party, although there is little immediate appetite for such a contentious policy at the current time, with the Prime

Minister engaged in delicate negotiations with other EU leaders over the future relationship between the UK and the rest of the EU. However, post-Brexit this may become a very real possibility.

The 'right to privacy'

One of the most contentious rights is the so-called 'right to privacy', which is expressed by the Convention in slightly different terms.

KEY STATUTE

Article 8 European Convention on Human Rights

1. Everyone has the right to respect for his private and family life, his home and his correspondence.

2. There shall be no interference by a public authority with the exercise of this right except such as is in accordance with the law and is necessary in a democratic society in the interests of national security, public safety or the economic well-being of the country, for the prevention of disorder or crime, for the protection of health or morals, or for the protection of the rights and freedoms of others.

Traditionally, the UK has avoided recognising a 'right to privacy', but has upheld the related concept of breach of confidence. Such actions do not address intrusion by the press, etc., but instead provide a remedy in those situations where a person has gained information as a result of a confidential relationship and later seeks to make that public (usually for financial gain). Increasingly, however, the doctrine of breach of confidence has been interpreted in a manner which resembles a right to privacy.

KEY CASE

Campbell v *Mirror Group Newspapers (MGN) Ltd* [2004] UKHL 22 (HL)

Concerning: right to privacy/breach of confidence

Facts

The defendant newspaper published details of model Naomi Campbell's drug treatment, including covertly taken photographs of her visits to Narcotics Anonymous meetings.

Legal principle

The court held that there was no pressing need for the publication, which was a clear violation of the model's right to privacy. Lord Hope: 'There was here an infringement of Miss Campbell's right to privacy that cannot be justified.'

KEY CASE

Douglas v *Hello Ltd* [2001] 2 All ER 289 (CA)

Concerning: right to privacy/breach of confidence

Facts

Photographs of the celebrity wedding of Michael Douglas and Catherine Zeta-Jones were to be published in *OK!* magazine under an exclusive agreement. A photographer took secret photos of the ceremony and sold them to the rival *Hello* magazine, which published them. Both the couple and *OK!* magazine sought damages from *Hello* for breach of confidence.

Legal principle

The court held that there had been a breach of the couple's confidence in the unauthorised publication of the pictures. Sedley LJ: 'The retained element of privacy, in the form of editorial control of *OK!*'s pictures, while real, is itself as much a commercial as a personal reservation.'

KEY CASE

HRH Prince of Wales v *Associated Newspapers Ltd* [2006] EWCA Civ 1776 (CA)

Concerning: right to privacy/breach of confidence

Facts

Private diaries of the Prince of Wales were copied by a member of his staff and passed to a newspaper, which published them. The published excerpts, written during a visit to Hong Kong in 1997, contained potentially embarrassing criticism by the Prince of the Chinese.

Legal principle

The court held that the member of staff was subject to a duty of confidence, which had been breached by the copying of the diaries and their subsequent publication. Lord Phillips CJ: 'Prince Charles had an unanswerable claim for breach of privacy. When the breach of a confidential relationship is added to the balance, his case is overwhelming.'

✎ EXAM TIP

Remember to make clear that, in the case of publication by newspapers, etc., there is a conflict between the Article 10 right of the media (the right to freedom of expression) and the Article 8 right of the individuals concerned. This requires a difficult balance to be established by the courts.

 Make your answer stand out

When discussing the issue of press intrusion and the right to privacy, include a brief mention of recent developments such as the use of so-called 'super injunctions' by celebrities to prevent reporting of personal matters, and the Leveson Inquiry into press intrusion and phone hacking. The final report can be found at:

http://webarchive.nationalarchives.gov.uk/20140122145147/http://www.official-documents.gov.uk/document/hc1213/hc07/0780/0780.asp

KEY CASE

Mosley v United Kingdom [2012] EMLR 1 (ECtHR)

Concerning: alleged breach of Article 8 (Right to Respect for Private Life)

Facts

The applicant alleged a breach of his Article 8 rights by the UK authorities in failing to require the *News of the World* to notify him in advance of publication of details about his private life so that he had an opportunity to seek an injunction to prevent publication.

Legal principle

Lech Garlicki (President): 'Article 8 does not require a legally binding pre-notification requirement. Accordingly . . . there has been no violation of Article 8 of the Convention by the absence of such a requirement in domestic law.'

Freedom of information and data protection

Although not 'privacy' in the strictest sense, the protection of personal data by the state and the access we are given to that information represents an emerging civil liberty which has been strengthened by statute in recent years.

Freedom of Information Act 2000, section 1

General right of access to information held by public authorities

Any person making a request for information to a public authority is entitled –

(a) to be informed in writing by the public authority whether it holds information of the description specified in the request, and

(b) if that is the case, to have that information communicated to him.

The 2000 Act requires public bodies to respond to requests for personal information within 20 working days, and operates under the supervision of the Information Commissioner. There are, however, potential exemptions from disclosure in relation to a number of categories of information, including those relating to:

■ security matters;

■ defence;

■ international relations;

■ the formulation of government policy.

Similar protections are provided by the Data Protection Act 1998, which regulates access to information contained in both computerised and manual files; this is supervised by the Data Protection Commissioner.

■ Putting it all together

Answer guidelines

See the essay question at the start of the chapter.

Approaching the question

■ Remember to address the three stages to the discussion: the original status of civil liberties in the UK as 'freedoms' rather than 'rights'; the process for enforcing Convention rights before the Human Rights Act 1998; and the position under the 1998 Act.

▶

Important points to include

■ Spend some time considering the distinction between 'rights' and 'freedoms', and the examples (such as the post-Dunblane handgun legislation) which show how easily so-called 'rights' can be removed.

■ Do not forget to emphasise the problems with the system before the Human Rights Act 1998, most notably the requirement to 'exhaust all domestic remedies' before being allowed to pursue a case in the Strasbourg Court.

■ Emphasise the greater role for the courts following the Human Rights Act 1998 and, in particular, the ability of the court to make a 'declaration of incompatibility'.

■ Always produce a conclusion which addresses the question. In this case that requires some assessment of whether the position of the individual citizen has been improved by the 1998 Act. On the basis that we can now enforce Convention rights in the UK courts, the answer is probably 'yes'.

 Make your answer stand out

■ Highlight the fact that successive governments in the UK had refused to incorporate the Convention into UK law before 1998, fearing a 'flood' of cases, which has not in fact materialised.

■ Emphasise the increased role of the courts under the Human Rights Act 1998, and the difference between the duty under section 3 of the Act and traditional statutory interpretation.

■ Note that this increased role for the courts does not threaten parliamentary sovereignty because Parliament can still refuse to amend legislation following a declaration of incompatibility.

READ TO IMPRESS

Arnull, A. (2003) From charter to constitution and beyond: fundamental rights in the new European Union. *Public Law*, 774–93.

Epstein, R. (2009) A bill of rights for the UK: has the time come? *Criminal Law and Justice Weekly*, 173: 8.

Hickman, T.R. (2005) Constitutional dialogue, constitutional theories and the Human Rights Act 1998. *Public Law*, 306–35.

Hiebert, J.L. (2012) Governing under the Human Rights Act: the limitations of wishful thinking. *Public Law,* 27–44.

Hohfeld, W. (1919) *Fundamental Legal Conceptions: As Applied in Judicial Reasoning.* New Haven: Yale University Press.

Kavanagh, A. (2006) The role of parliamentary intention in adjudication under the Human Rights Act 1998. *Oxford Journal of Legal Studies,* 26: 179–206.

Klug, F. and Starmer, K. (2005) Standing back from the Human Rights Act: how effective is it five years on? *Public Law,* 716–28.

Klug, F. and Wildbore, H. (2007) Breaking new ground: the Joint Committee on Human Rights and the role of parliament in human rights compliance. *European Human Rights Law Review,* 3: 231–50.

Lord Lester of Herne Hill (2012) The European Court of Human Rights and the Human Rights Act: British concerns. *Judicial Review,* 17(1): 1–10.

Nicol, D. (2006) Law and politics after the Human Rights Act. *Public Law,* 722–51.

Steyn, Lord (2005) 2000–2005: Laying the foundations of human rights law in the United Kingdom. *European Human Rights Law Review,* 4: 349–62.

www.pearsoned.co.uk/lawexpress

 Go online to access more revision support including quizzes to test your knowledge, sample questions with answer guidelines, printable versions of the topic maps, and more!

Freedom of expression and assembly

7

Revision checklist

Essential points you should know:

- [ ] Some of the major restrictions on the right to freedom of expression in the UK
- [ ] The nature of public protest and the distinction between assemblies and processions
- [ ] The powers of the police in relation to the supervision and control of public assemblies
- [ ] The powers of the police in relation to the supervision and control of public processions

■ Topic map

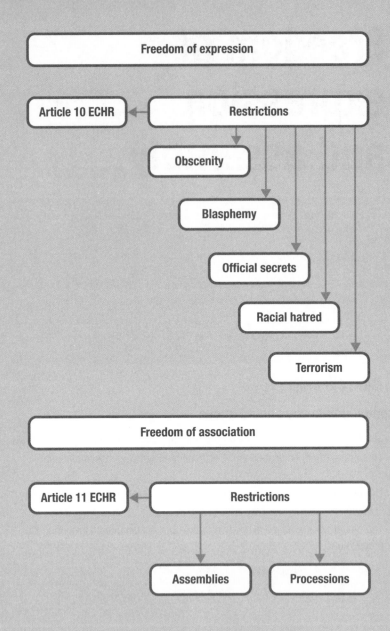

A printable version of this topic map is available from **www.pearsoned.co.uk/lawexpress**

■ Introduction

We may have a right to freedom of expression, but that does not mean that we can say what we like when we like.

Freedom of expression and freedom of assembly are seen as two of the most fundamental civil liberties, allowing us to speak freely and to protest publicly. However, these rights are not absolute and there are a number of restrictions on what we can say and how we can protest on the streets. Such restrictions illustrate the conflict between the civil liberties of the individual and the powers of the state. For this reason the topic is always popular with examiners.

ASSESSMENT ADVICE

Essay questions

Essay questions on freedom of expression will usually ask you to provide an overview of the restrictions placed on free speech in the UK. Less common are questions which ask you to concentrate on one specific area, such as blasphemy or issues of race and religion. In all cases, remember not just to list the provisions but also to include some analysis of the supposed justification for state restrictions on free speech. Even a modest level of evaluation will gain you valuable extra marks.

Problem questions

Problem questions on freedom of association are always popular and usually require you to apply public order legislation to a scenario, typically an assembly or procession. Here the key is to be methodical and work through the relevant provisions, demonstrating how they relate to the facts of the question. Do not fall into the trap of jumping to the end and making suggestions as to how to control a public meeting without first showing that you have applied the relevant provisions and the tests which they contain.

■ Sample question

Could you answer this question? Below is a typical problem question that could arise on this topic. Guidelines on answering the question are included at the end of this chapter, whilst a sample essay question and guidance on tackling it can be found on the companion website.

PROBLEM QUESTION

Fircombe is an inner-city estate which achieved notoriety last year following a weekend of racially motivated rioting, and, although everyone has worked hard to establish some sense of community, there is still tension on the estate. Four houses in Jubilee Street are owned by Joshua Fiddler, a slum landlord, who has recently let them to families who have been evicted from local authority accommodation due to anti-social behaviour. Their children have quickly established themselves with a spate of burglaries and car thefts, and relations in the street are strained.

On Monday 21 June two of the youths steal a car and drive to the neighbouring Newcombe estate, which is predominantly Asian. During a police pursuit they lose control of the car, which mounts the pavement, seriously injuring a local man. The youths are arrested and when they are brought before the magistrates the following day bail is refused. Their families are furious and there is a disturbance in the court. Later that day the police receive reports that witnesses to the car crash have been threatened.

On the morning of Wednesday 23 June the local man dies in hospital and, at the local police station, Superintendent Ellis receives a telephone call from Newcombe's community leaders, Anil and Sunil, who inform him that, because of the man's death, they have decided to bring forward July's annual Asian Pride march and hold it on Saturday 26 June instead. They provide Supt Ellis with a proposed route for the procession which, as in previous years, will circle their estate. This takes the march along Warwick Street, which marks the boundary between the Newcombe and Fircombe estates. However, unknown to Supt Ellis, Anil and Sunil plan to change the route on the day to take the march down Jubilee Street.

On Wednesday evening, Supt Ellis learns that one of the youths has committed suicide in prison.

Advise Anil and Sunil on their obligations under public order legislation.

Advise Supt Ellis of the steps he can take to defuse the situation.

■ Freedom of expression

Freedom of expression (or freedom of speech) is seen as one of the most important of our civil liberties. It is safeguarded by Article 10 of the European Convention on Human Rights.

> **!** Don't be tempted to . . .
>
> ## Freedom of expression and Article 10
>
> Students frequently make the mistake of thinking that Article 10 guarantees free speech, but this is not the case. Look at the wording of Article 10 below and you will see that, as with many of the other rights guaranteed under the Convention, the state is still able to impose restrictions under certain circumstances.

KEY STATUTE

European Convention on Human Rights, Article 10

Everyone has the right to freedom of expression. This right shall include freedom to hold opinions and to receive and impart information and ideas without interference by public authority.

However, Article 10 continues to state that this right:

. . . may be subject to such formalities, conditions, restrictions or penalties as are pre-scribed by law and are necessary in a democratic society.

This means that the state can restrict free speech, providing that this is done in accordance with either statute or common law. There are a number of such restrictions, including the laws relating to obscenity, blasphemy and official secrets, together with more recent provisions relating to terrorism. Not all cases, however, concern the written or spoken word.

KEY CASE

Gough v *United Kingdom* **(2014) 38 BHRC 281 (ECtHR)**

Concerning: Article 10

Facts

The applicant firmly believed in the inoffensiveness of the human body, which he expressed by being naked in public. Owing to his refusal to wear clothes in public he was repeatedly arrested, prosecuted, convicted and imprisoned for the offence of breach of the peace. He complained that this violated his rights to privacy and freedom of expression.

Legal principle

Held. The applicant's public nudity could be seen as a form of expression which fell within the ambit of Article 10 and so his arrest, prosecution, conviction and detention constituted an interference with his exercise of his right to freedom of expression. ▶

However, these actions by the state were aimed to ensure respect for the law and to prevent the disorder which would potentially ensue were the applicant permitted continually and persistently to go nude in public. The measures adopted by the police, the prosecuting authorities and the courts were 'relevant and sufficient' and the measures met a pressing social need in response to repeated anti-social conduct by the applicant. It followed that there was no violation of Article 10. Judge Ziemele: 'Article 10 does not go so far as to enable individuals, even those sincerely convinced of the virtue of their own beliefs, to repeatedly impose their anti-social conduct on other, unwilling members of society and then to claim a disproportionate interference with the exercise of their freedom of expression when the state, in the performance of its duty to protect the public from public nuisances, enforces the law in respect of such deliberately repetitive anti-social conduct.'

☐ REVISION NOTE

When revising freedom of expression, remember to include the section on contempt of court in Chapter 4, as this is another important restriction on freedom of speech.

Obscenity

KEY STATUTE

Obscene Publications Act 1959, sections 1(1), 2(1)

For the purposes of this Act an article shall be deemed to be obscene if its effect . . . is, if taken as a whole, such as to tend to deprave and corrupt . . .

. . . any person who, whether for gain or not, publishes an obscene article [or who has an obscene article for publication for gain (whether gain to himself or gain to another)] shall be liable.

KEY CASE

DPP v *Whyte* [1972] AC 849 (HL)

Concerning: meaning of 'tend to deprave and corrupt'

Facts

A husband and wife ran a bookshop which was raided by police who seized a large amount of pornography. It was argued that the customers of the shop could not be 'depraved and corrupted' by the pornography sold by the couple because they were already used to viewing such material.

Legal principle

It was held that there was nothing in the wording of the Act which justified the defendants' assertions. Lord Wilberforce: 'the Act is not merely concerned with the once and for all corruption of the wholly innocent; it equally protects the less innocent from further corruption'.

KEY CASE

Calder (John) (Publications) Ltd v *Powell* [1965] 1 QB 509 (QB)

Concerning: meaning of 'tend to deprave and corrupt'

Facts

A book was published depicting the life of a drug addict and highlighting the 'favourable' aspects of drug taking.

Legal principle

It was held that obscenity was not exclusively confined to sexual matters. A book encouraging drug abuse could equally be termed 'obscene'. Lord Parker CJ: 'In my judgment there is no reason whatever to confine obscenity and depravity to sex, and there was ample evidence upon which the justices could hold that this book was obscene.'

 Make your answer stand out

Note that the wider concept of 'obscenity' now includes the possession and distribution of indecent 'pseudo-photographs' of children under s. 1 of the Protection of Children Act 1978. See *R* v *Gojkovic (Mihajlo)* [2017] EWCA Crim 1025.

Note also the related, but little used, common law offences of 'conspiracy to corrupt public morals' and 'conspiracy to outrage public decency'.

KEY CASE

Shaw v *DPP* [1962] AC 220 (HL)

Concerning: conspiracy to corrupt public morals

Facts

The defendant published a magazine containing contact details for prostitutes. ▶

Legal principle

The House of Lords held that a conviction was justified. Viscount Simonds: 'There remains in the courts of law a residual power to enforce the supreme and fundamental purpose of the law, to conserve not only the safety and order but also the moral welfare of the state.'

KEY CASE

R v Gibson [1990] 2 QB 619 (CA)

Concerning: conspiracy to outrage public decency

Facts

The defendant staged an art exhibition containing a work made from a model head wearing two earrings, each made from a frozen three-month-old human foetus.

Legal principle

Regardless of whether there was a 'tendency to deprave and corrupt', an offence was committed where a public exhibition outraged public decency. Lord Lane CJ: 'The object of the common law offence is to protect the public from suffering feelings of outrage by such exhibition.'

Blasphemy

Another restriction on freedom of expression is the common law offence of blasphemy, roughly defined as statements which are insulting or abusive to Christian belief. Although there are few modern prosecutions for blasphemy, it remains a possible charge.

KEY CASE

R v Lemon [1979] AC 617 (HL)

Concerning: intention and blasphemy

Facts

The magazine *Gay News* published a poem depicting the life of Jesus and describing sexual acts committed on his body after crucifixion.

Legal principle

There was no requirement for an intention to blaspheme. All that was needed was the publication of material which was later held to be blasphemous. Viscount Dilhorne: 'The harm is done by their intentional publication, whether or not the publisher intended to blaspheme.'

KEY CASE

R v *Chief Metropolitan Stipendary Magistrate, ex parte Choudhury* **[1991] 1 QB 429 (QB)**

Concerning: blasphemy and other religions

Facts

The claimant alleged that the novel *The Satanic Verses* by the author Salman Rushdie was blasphemous against Islam.

Legal principle

The court held that the offence of blasphemy could only be committed against Christianity. Watkins LJ: 'We have no doubt that as the law now stands it does not extend to religions other than Christianity.'

Official secrets

There are also offences arising from the disclosure of official secrets. This is now covered by the Official Secrets Act 1989, which creates a range of offences.

Offences under the Official Secrets Act 1989

A member (or former member) of the security or intelligence services	' . . . if without lawful authority he discloses any information, document or other article relating to security or intelligence which is or has been in his possession by virtue of his position as a member of any of those services'. (section 1(1))
A person who is or has been a Crown servant or government contractor	' . . . if without lawful authority he makes a damaging disclosure of any information, document or other article relating to security or intelligence which is or has been in his possession by virtue of his position'. (section 1(3))
	' . . . if without lawful authority he makes a damaging disclosure of any information, document or other article relating to defence which is or has been in his possession by virtue of his position'. (section 2(1))
	' . . . if without lawful authority he makes a damaging disclosure of any information, document or other article relating to international relations . . . which is or has been in his possession by virtue of his position'. (section 3(1))

(continued)

' . . . if without lawful authority he discloses any information . . . which is or has been in his possession by virtue of his position . . . which –

(i)   results in the commission of an offence;

(ii) facilitates an escape from legal custody;

(iii) impedes the prevention or detection of offences'. (section 4)

KEY CASE

Secretary of State for Defence v *Guardian Newspapers Ltd* **[1985] AC 339 (HL)**

Concerning: disclosure of official secrets

Facts

Sarah Tisdall, who worked in the Foreign Office, revealed to the *Guardian* newspaper the secret arrival of American nuclear missiles at a UK airforce base. Tisdall claimed that revealing this information was in the public interest.

Legal principle

It was held that she had contravened the Official Secrets Act and she was sentenced to six months' imprisonment. Lord Roskill: 'it was necessary in the interests of national security that that document should be delivered up [by the newspaper] in order that the offender might be identified'.

KEY CASE

R v *Ponting* **[1985] Crim LR 318 (CCC)**

Concerning: disclosure of official secrets

Facts

Clive Ponting, an official within the Ministry of Defence, sent documents to an MP confirming that the government had misled Parliament over the sinking of the ship the *General Belgrano* during the Falklands War, with the death of 368 sailors. He was subsequently prosecuted under the Official Secrets Act.

Legal principle

The case was clearly proven and the judge directed the jury to convict but, instead, they acquitted Ponting, believing his claim that the disclosure was in the public interest.

Don't be tempted to . . .

Official Secrets Act 1911 and Official Secrets Act 1989

When discussing these cases, be sure to point out that both Tisdall and Ponting were charged under the Official Secrets Act 1911, which was later amended by the Official Secrets Act 1989.

✓ Make your answer stand out

The current provisions on official secrets continue to cause concern, with the fear that the state will use the law to prevent not only the disclosure of secrets, but also information which is simply embarrassing to the government, and any examination answer should emphasise such concern. For a discussion of some of the cases in this area, see Bindham (2007). You might also demonstrate an awareness of recent events surrounding the American whistleblower Edward Snowden, who leaked details of a mass surveillance programme by the USA security services. Demonstrate your up-to-date knowledge by mentioning the recent case of *Privacy International* v *Secretary of State for Foreign and Commonwealth Affairs and others* [2016] UKIPTrib 15_110-CH, which saw an unsuccessful challenge to gathering of 'bulk' personal data by the security services.

Incitement to racial hatred

Further restrictions of freedom of expression have been introduced to combat racial and religious abuse.

KEY STATUTE

Public Order Act 1986, sections 18(1), 19(1)

A person who uses threatening, abusive or insulting words or behaviour, or displays any written material which is threatening, abusive or insulting, is guilty of an offence if –

(a) he intends thereby to stir up racial hatred, or

(b) having regard to all the circumstances racial hatred is likely to be stirred up thereby.

A person who publishes or distributes written material which is threatening, abusive or insulting is guilty of an offence if –

(a) he intends thereby to stir up racial hatred, or

(b) having regard to all the circumstances racial hatred is likely to be stirred up thereby.

Similar provisions in relation to religious hatred have been introduced by the Racial and Religious Hatred Act 2006.

Terrorism legislation

Restrictions on freedom of expression are also contained within current terrorism legislation.

KEY STATUTE

Terrorism Act 2000, section 12(3)

A person commits an offence if he addresses a meeting and the purpose of his address is to encourage support for a proscribed organisation or to further its activities.

✓ Make your answer stand out

Make clear to the examiner that you are also aware of more recent anti-terrorism legislation, such as the Counter-Terrorism and Security Act 2015, which also has freedom of speech implications, not least by placing a responsibility on schools to participate in work to prevent people from being drawn into terrorism, and to challenge extremist ideas that support or are shared by terrorist groups.

Freedom of association

Closely related to freedom of speech is the freedom of association – the freedom to protest in groups. This protest takes two forms: assemblies and processions. As with freedom of expression, freedom of association is protected under the European Convention, but with similar limitations.

KEY STATUTE

European Convention on Human Rights, Article 11

Everyone has the right to freedom of peaceful assembly and to freedom of association with others . . .

However, Article 11 continues:

. . . this article shall not prevent the imposition of lawful restrictions on the exercise of these rights by members of the armed forces, of the police or of the administration of the State.

Assemblies

An assembly is defined as 'an assembly of 2 or more persons in a public place which is wholly or partly open to the air' (Public Order Act 1986, section 16). The Act allows the police to impose conditions on assemblies where certain conditions are satisfied.

KEY STATUTE

Public Order Act 1986, section 14(1)

If the senior police officer, having regard to the time or place at which and the circumstances in which any public assembly is being held or is intended to be held, reasonably believes that –

(a) it may result in serious public disorder, serious damage to property or serious disruption to the life of the community, or

(b) the purpose of the persons organising it is the intimidation of others with a view to compelling them not to do an act they have a right to do, or to do an act they have a right not to do,

he may give directions imposing on the persons organising or taking part in the assembly such conditions as to the place at which the assembly may be (or continue to be) held, its maximum duration, or the maximum number of persons who may constitute it, as appear to him necessary to prevent such disorder, damage, disruption or intimidation.

In this way, if the police believe that there will be serious public disorder, serious damage to property, etc., conditions can be imposed on the assembly.

EXAM TIP

Although this is the most commonly used power to control assemblies, you can also mention the ban on protests in the vicinity of Parliament under section 132 of the Serious Organised Crime and Police Act 2005 and the control on assemblies which trespass on land under section 14A of the Public Order Act 1986.

Processions

KEY CASE

Flockhart v *Robinson* [1950] 2 KB 498 (DC)

Concerning: definition of a 'procession'

Facts

The defendant was accused of organising a political procession. This required the court to define what was meant in law by the term 'procession'. ▶

> **Legal principle**
>
> Lord Goddard CJ: 'A procession is not a mere body of persons: it is a body of persons moving along a route.'

The situation in relation to processions is more complex, but the basic principle is the same as for assemblies. If the police are satisfied that there is a risk of certain consequences, conditions can be imposed and (in extreme cases) the procession can be banned. With processions, the question of notice must also be considered. In this way, there are three stages to considering a question on processions:

1. Has proper notice been given by the organisers to the police?
2. Are there grounds for imposing conditions on the procession?
3. What conditions could be imposed to remove the risk of disorder?

! Don't be tempted to . . .

Processions

Many students trip up in examinations when answering questions on processions by immediately suggesting the imposition of conditions. Remember, the right to freedom of association should only be limited where absolutely necessary. Therefore, begin any answer from the position that the procession should be allowed to proceed unchanged unless this will result in disorder. If this is not possible, then the aim is to impose the *minimum* conditions necessary to remove the threat to public order.

Has proper notice been given by the organisers to the police?

Before we can answer this question we need to know whether the procession in question is one which is covered by the 1986 Act.

KEY STATUTE

> **Public Order Act 1986, section 11**
>
> (1) Written notice shall be given in accordance with this section of any proposal to hold a public procession intended –
>
>   (a) to demonstrate support for or opposition to the views or actions of any person or body of persons,
>
>   (b) to publicise a cause or campaign, or
>
>   (c) to mark or commemorate an event, unless it is not reasonably practicable to give any advance notice of the procession.

(2) Subsection (1) does not apply where the procession is one commonly or customarily held in the police area (or areas) in which it is proposed to be held or is a funeral procession organised by a funeral director acting in the normal course of his business.

(3) The notice must specify the date when it is intended to hold the procession, the time when it is intended to start it, its proposed route, and the name and address of the person (or of one of the persons) proposing to organise it.

Therefore, the notice requirements can be summarised as follows, depending on the purpose of the procession:

Notice required	Notice not required
Support or opposition for the views or actions of a person or persons	Commonly or customarily held procession
Publicise cause or campaign	Funerals
Mark or commemorate an event	

✎ EXAM TIP

There is clearly a potential overlap between a procession to mark or commemorate an event (which requires notice) and a customarily held procession (which does not), and examiners will credit any recognition of this dilemma. Point out that the solution is to consider the other grounds as well to see if these are satisfied (e.g. publicise a cause or campaign).

Notice

The notice must specify:

- date and time of procession;
- route;
- names of organisers.

The notice must be delivered to the police six days before the procession. Failure to provide notice is an offence. Note that the notice requirement applies only where this is 'reasonably practicable', so consider whether it is possible for the organisers to give notice (e.g. if the procession is a spontaneous reaction to events).

It is also an offence to deviate from the details contained in the notice (time, route, etc.) unless this is beyond the control of the organisers.

Are there grounds for imposing conditions on the procession?

Once notice has been received, the police assess whether the procession can proceed as planned. This is done by reference to section 12 of the 1986 Act.

KEY STATUTE

Public Order Act 1986, section 12(1)

If the senior police officer, having regard to the time or place at which and the circumstances in which any public procession is being held or is intended to be held and to its route or proposed route, reasonably believes that –

(a) it may result in serious public disorder, serious damage to property or serious disruption to the life of the community, or

(b) the purpose of the persons organising it is the intimidation of others with a view to compelling them not to do an act they have a right to do, or to do an act they have a right not to do,

he may give directions imposing on the persons organising or taking part in the procession such conditions as appear to him necessary to prevent such disorder, damage, disruption or intimidation, including conditions as to the route of the procession or prohibiting it from entering any public place specified in the directions.

Conditions might include:

■ changing the date/time of the procession;

■ changing the route to avoid potential confrontation.

Banning processions

If the powers under section 12 are thought insufficient to prevent disorder, the police can apply to ban all processions in the area for a maximum of three months.

KEY STATUTE

Public Order Act 1986, section 13(1)

If at any time the chief officer of police reasonably believes that . . . the powers under section 12 will not be sufficient to prevent . . . serious public disorder, he shall apply to the council of the district for an order prohibiting for such period not exceeding 3 months . . . the holding of all public processions (or of any class of public procession so specified) in the district or part concerned.

Note that any ban affects *all* processions in the area, not just the one which formed the basis of the application/notice. This prevents the original organisation from simply changing its name in order to avoid the ban.

✎ EXAM TIP

Although you should mention the possibility of a ban in any answer, it should be emphasised as the last resort for the police. Remember, the objective is to balance freedom of speech and public order – banning the procession (and freedom of speech) is a drastic measure not to be taken lightly, so make sure the examiner appreciates that you understand this point.

It should also be noted that the recent Anti-social Behaviour, Crime and Policing Act 2014 also has potential implications for public order policing and freedom of expression, as illustrated by the following decision.

KEY CASE

Chief Constable of the Bedfordshire Police v *Golding and another* [2015] EWHC 1875 (QB)

Concerning: Anti-Social Behaviour, Crime and Policing Act 2014

Facts

The Chief Constable of Bedfordshire Police applied for injunctions against the group 'Britain First' to prevent them from marching through Luton on Saturday 27 June 2015, a day which was not only during the month of Ramadan, but was also the day scheduled for a community celebration known as 'Luton in Harmony'. Under section 1 of the Anti-social Behaviour, Crime and Policing Act 2014, the court may grant an injunction if satisfied, on the balance of probabilities, that the Respondent has engaged or threatens to engage in anti-social behaviour and the court considers it just and convenient to grant the injunction for the purpose of preventing the Respondent from engaging in anti-social behaviour.

Legal principle

The injunctions would be granted. Knowles J: 'Of course "Britain First" comes across as fundamentally and obviously wrong. In these times, which are troubled times . . . The police have the hardest job in dealing with it, nationally and locally. And so does the Council, locally.'

■ Putting it all together

Answer guidelines

See the problem question at the start of the chapter.

Approaching the question

- As with all examination questions which involve the application of statutory provisions to a scenario, you need to establish the relevant sections of the Act that apply and then work through the various requirements of each section.
- Remember to address any possible defences and areas of uncertainty in the facts as provided.
- Always offer some advice to the parties concerned.

Important points to include

You need to adopt a methodical approach to such questions, dealing with the following points in turn:

- Is this a 'procession' for the purposes of the 1986 Act? Almost all processions are covered but you need to show that you have established this point.
- Has adequate notice been served on the police? This should be done unless not 'reasonably practicable'.
- Do the circumstances suggest that conditions will be required?
- What are the minimum conditions required to remove the threat to public order?
- As a last resort, is a ban needed?

 Make your answer stand out

- Show that you can balance the competing requirements of legitimate protest and public order. In this scenario, changing the route of the procession might prevent disorder, but a procession which does not go anywhere near those with different views is unlikely to influence anything. Emphasise that you understand the dilemma this poses.
- Show that you have worked through the questions in turn – do not jump in with 'the procession could be banned'.
- Do not just state that conditions could be imposed – suggest what they might be (e.g. change of date/time, change of route, etc.).

READ TO IMPRESS

Bindham, J. (2007) Blowing the right whistle. *New Law Journal,* 157: 602.

Burrows, D. (2017) Contempt and court proceedings (Pt 1). *New Law Journal,* 7728: 12.

Hamilton, M. (2007) Freedom of assembly, consequential harms and the rule of law: liberty-limiting principles in the context of transition. *Oxford Journal of Legal Studies,* 27: 75–100.

Jaconelli, J. (2007) Defences to speech crimes. *European Human Rights Law Review,* 1: 27–46.

James, J. and Ghandi, S. (1998) The English law of blasphemy and the European Convention on Human Rights. *European Human Rights Law Review,* 4: 430–51.

Kearns, P. (2000) Obscene and blasphemous libel: misunderstanding art. *Criminal Law Review,* 652–60.

Loveland, I. (2001) Freedom of political expression: who needs the Human Rights Act? *Public Law,* 233–44.

Sherlock, A. (1995) Freedom of expression: how far should it go? *European Law Review,* 20(3): 329–37.

Smartt, U. (2011) Twitter undermines superinjunctions. *Communications Law,* 16(4): 135–39.

www.pearsoned.co.uk/lawexpress

 Go online to access more revision support including quizzes to test your knowledge, sample questions with answer guidelines, printable versions of the topic maps, and more!

Police powers

8

Revision checklist

Essential points you should know:

- [ ] The constitutional status of police powers
- [ ] The importance and main scope of the Police and Criminal Evidence Act 1984 (PACE) and Codes of Practice
- [ ] Powers of arrest available to police officers and the public
- [ ] Powers of stop search and search of premises available to police officers
- [ ] Legal requirements relating to police detention and questioning

■ Topic map

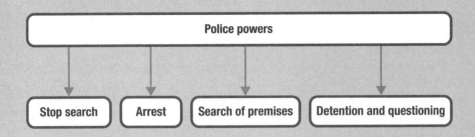

■ Introduction

Police powers are the most visible example of the power of the state being used against the individual.

In Chapter 6 we considered the balance between the interests of the state and the civil liberties of the individual. Police powers represent one of the most important and most commonly used areas of state power. The police are one of the few elements of the state which are authorised to use force against the general public, and so it is essential that police powers are clearly defined and controlled. The constitutional importance of police powers makes the topic a favourite with examiners.

ASSESSMENT ADVICE

Essay questions

Essay questions on police powers can focus on a number of areas. Questions may ask you to consider whether the police have too much power, or, alternatively, whether additional powers are needed. Questions might also ask you to assess the effectiveness of PACE 1984 in regulating police powers and preventing the abuse of power by officers. Such essays require not only a sound knowledge of the provisions, but also a critical approach to the purpose and function of police powers. Remember that examiners are always looking for analysis and evaluation as well as mere description of the law.

Problem questions

Problem questions on police powers are much more common and can focus on any of the key areas, such as stop search, arrest, search of premises and the detention and questioning of suspects. Often questions will require you to consider a chain of events from initial contact, stop search and arrest, through to detention and questioning. In all cases, a clear knowledge of the relevant sections of PACE is essential, together with a methodical approach to applying the provisions. The key to answering such questions is to work through the events, addressing the issues as they arise.

■ Sample question

Could you answer this question? Below is a typical problem question that could arise on this topic. Guidelines on answering the question are included at the end of this chapter, whilst a sample essay question and guidance on tackling it can be found on the companion website.

PROBLEM QUESTION

Barbara is a pensioner who returned home some weeks ago to find a burglar in her house. The man ran off but Barbara was able to give the police a detailed description of a pale, thin man in his early 20s, with short, cropped fair hair. The man swore at her as he left and, consequently, she has also been able to tell the police that he had a Scottish accent. As there has been a spate of such burglaries in the area, the police have ensured that officers patrolling the area are aware of the description.

At 11.30 p.m., police constables Bradshaw and Smith see Kenny, a local youth with previous convictions for indecent exposure and assault, entering the street where Barbara lives. He is carrying a holdall. The officers recognise him instantly due to his long black hair and, when stopped and questioned, he tells them that he has been to the pub and is on his way to stay with a friend who lives nearby.

PC Bradshaw tells him that he is suspected of burglary and asks him to turn out his pockets, but Kenny refuses. At this, PC Smith snatches the holdall from Kenny and PC Bradshaw marches him into a nearby empty bus shelter, where he is ordered to remove his coat, shirt and shoes while Smith blocks the doorway. Although the search of Kenny's clothing reveals nothing, Bradshaw finds a screwdriver and a pair of gloves in the holdall. Kenny explains that his friend asked him to bring the screwdriver as he wanted to borrow it to fix his washing machine.

Kenny is taken to his friend's house, which is empty, and the police conduct a search after forcing an entry to the premises. In one of the bedrooms they find a small quantity of amphetamines and Kenny is arrested.

Assess the legality of the actions of the officers in this case.

▇ Police powers

Police powers are simply a way for the law to authorise conduct which would otherwise be illegal. For example, holding someone against their will would normally be false imprisonment, but the powers of arrest available under the 1984 Police and Criminal Evidence Act (PACE) and other Acts of Parliament provide lawful authority for detaining the person.

Police and Criminal Evidence Act 1984 (PACE)

Any student hoping to answer examination questions on police powers must be familiar with the main provisions of the Police and Criminal Evidence Act 1984 (PACE). The Act governs all aspects of police contact with a suspect, from conducting stop search in the street to detention and questioning at the police station. The Act also has a small number of provisions which affect the presentation (and exclusion) of police evidence in court. Some of the key areas covered by PACE include:

Sections	Regulating
ss. 1–5	Stop search of persons and vehicles
ss. 8–23 and s. 32	Search of premises
ss. 24–31	Powers of arrest
ss. 34–65	Detention and questioning of suspects
s. 76	Confession evidence
s. 78	Exclusion of evidence at court

Codes of Practice

In addition to the provisions of PACE itself, there are also the Codes of Practice which contain the detailed rules governing key areas of police powers. These are divided into Codes of Practice A to H.

Code of Practice	Regulating
A	Stop search powers
B	Search of premises
C	Detention and questioning
D	Identification procedures
E	Tape recording of interviews
F	Visual recording of interviews
G	Powers of arrest
H	Detention and questioning in terrorism cases

✎ EXAM TIP

Although examination answers will focus on the provisions of PACE, do not forget to mention the Codes of Practice and emphasise their importance. Examiners will give credit for an appreciation of the relationship between the statutory provisions and the Codes of Practice. This is particularly important in areas such as detention and questioning, where a failure to adequately follow the Codes of Practice may render any subsequent confession inadmissible as evidence in court. You should also emphasise that the Codes are subject to periodic revision. See Zander (2013).

Background to PACE

The 1984 Act was introduced in response to widespread concern over the abuse of police powers in the early 1980s, which culminated in a series of riots. The subsequent Scarman Report made a number of recommendations regarding police powers, many of which were incorporated into PACE 1984.

 Make your answer stand out

Although it is unlikely that you would face a question on the background to PACE, examiners will be impressed by any indication that you understand why PACE came into being and the tensions which underpin police powers. See the Scarman Report (1981). Similarly, demonstrating an awareness of more recent developments in the area will always enhance your answer. For example, you might mention that, in January 2012, the successful conviction of two men for the racially motivated murder of black teenager Stephen Lawrence led to a further review of the use of police stop search powers to prevent their disproportionate use against certain groups within the community.

KEY CASE

Rice v *Connolly* [1966] 2 QB 414 (QB)

Concerning: the obligation to assist the police

Facts

A man was found by the police in an area where burglaries had occurred. When questioned, he refused to explain his presence or give his name and address. He was subsequently arrested for obstructing the police.

Legal principle

It was held that, although every citizen had a moral or social duty to assist the police, there was no relevant legal duty to that effect. Therefore, he had been entitled to decline to answer the questions put to him and (prior to his arrest) to accompany the police officer on request. Lord Parker CJ: 'There is all the difference in the world between deliberately telling a false story – something which on no view a citizen has a right to do – and preserving silence or refusing to answer – something which he has every right to do.'

Stop search

The power to stop someone in the street and search them against their will has always been one of the most contentious police powers because, historically, people from ethnic minorities have been statistically more likely to be stop searched by the police. This led to calls for greater control over these powers.

Stop search is authorised by section 1 of PACE, which applies to the search of people and of vehicles. However, this only permits the police to search where there is a reasonable suspicion that certain specified objects will be found. Code A, governing stop and search, has recently been revised to clarify what can and cannot constitute reasonable grounds for suspicion justifying a search.

KEY STATUTE

PACE, Code of Practice A

2:2 This test . . . is in two parts:

(i) *Firstly,* the officer must have formed a *genuine* suspicion in their own mind that they will find the object for which the search power being exercised allows them to search; and

(ii) *Secondly,* the suspicion that the object will be found must be reasonable. This means that there must be an *objective* basis for that suspicion based on facts, information and/or intelligence which are relevant to the likelihood that the object in question will be found, so that a reasonable person would be entitled to reach the same conclusion based on the same facts and information and/or intelligence.

! Don't be tempted to . . .

The nature of stop search

Students frequently make the mistake in examinations of not recognising that a search is only lawful when it is based on the reasonable suspicion that prohibited items will be found. In this way, the police cannot search to generate the reasonable suspicion – they must have the reasonable suspicion first.

What items justify a stop search?

Under section 1 of PACE, a search is authorised if the officer has reasonable suspicion that the person or vehicle is carrying one of the following prohibited items:

- stolen items;
- offensive weapons;
- items intended for use in the commission of burglary, theft, deception, criminal damage or taking a vehicle without consent;
- fireworks.

What constitutes 'reasonable suspicion'?

This can be difficult to establish but is important – if the officer does not have reasonable suspicion then the search may be unlawful.

KEY STATUTE

PACE Code of Practice A

2.2B Reasonable suspicion can never be supported on the basis of personal factors. This means that unless the police have information or intelligence which *provides a description* of a person suspected of carrying an article for which there is a power to stop and search, the following *cannot be used*, alone or in combination with each other, or in combination with any other factor, as the reason for stopping and searching any individual, including any vehicle which they are driving or are being carried in:

(a) A person's physical appearance with regard, for example, to any of the 'relevant protected characteristics' set out in the Equality Act 2010, section 149, which are age, disability, gender reassignment, pregnancy and maternity, race, religion or belief, sex and sexual orientation . . . or the fact that the person is known to have a previous conviction; and

(b) Generalisations or stereotypical images that certain groups or categories of people are more likely to be involved in criminal activity.

❗ Don't be tempted to . . .

Previous convictions

It is very common for students to state that previous convictions justify a stop search – this is not so. Under PACE, the fact that a person has previous convictions for theft is not enough for the police to search them to see whether they are carrying stolen property.

Where can a person be searched?

The powers under section 1 of PACE are 'street powers' (i.e. designed to be used on the street, not in the police station) and can only be exercised in a place where the public have access, by right or by permission (whether for payment or not). The powers do not apply in private dwellings. They also do not apply in the gardens of private dwellings, unless the officer has reasonable grounds to believe that the person to be searched is not the occupier of the house and is not there with the occupier's permission.

What can be searched?

As a 'street power', the search under section 1 is superficial and does not involve removing clothing. Therefore, an officer can only order a person to remove outer clothing, such as an outer coat, jacket or gloves.

What information must be given?

Before conducting the search, the officer must give the person being searched the following information:

- the officer's police station and name;
- the object of the search (i.e. what the officer believes the person is carrying);
- the grounds for the search (i.e. why this person is being searched and not someone else).

The person who has been searched is entitled to a record of the search unless exceptional circumstances make this impractical. For example, if the encounter takes place amid public disorder or the officer is urgently called away to deal with an emergency.

 Make your answer stand out

In any answer which mentions stop search, make clear that there are now also provisions for 'suspicionless' stop search under s. 60 of the Criminal Justice and Public Order Act 1994, although this can only be authorised for a maximum period of 24 hours is a designated area where a senior police officer reasonably believes that serious ▶

violence may take place. See *R (on the application of Roberts)* v *Metropolitan Police Commissioner and another* [2015] UKSC 79 for an examination of these powers by the Supreme Court.

■ Powers of arrest

The power of arrest is one of the most important police powers because it deprives a person of their liberty. Unlike stop search powers, which are available only to police officers, there are also powers of arrest available to the public: so-called 'citizen's arrest'. Therefore, in answering any question on arrest, you must first establish whether the person making the arrest is a police officer or not. This determines which powers should be applied. (Note that here we are discussing arrest *without* warrant. An arrest under warrant would never be made by a member of the public and so the distinction between the powers available to police officers and other persons does not arise in such cases.) A warrant would be issued, for example, by the court where a person fails to appear for a court hearing.

✎ EXAM TIP

You should view powers of arrest as a two-tier system: there are general powers of arrest which are available to everyone (PACE, section 24A) and an additional set of powers which are available *only* to police officers (PACE, section 24).

Powers of arrest available to members of the public

Whereas a police officer can make an arrest in relation to any offence, a member of the public can make an arrest only in relation to an indictable offence. Also, a member of the public cannot make an arrest in the belief that an offence is going to be committed – their powers of arrest only apply where:

■ an offence *is being* committed (where a member of the public can arrest someone committing the offence or whom they have reasonable grounds to suspect is committing the offence); or

■ an offence *has been* committed (where a member of the public can arrest someone who has committed the offence or whom they have reasonable grounds to suspect has committed the offence).

Note that the powers of arrest available to the general public apply only where an actual offence is committed – if no offence has been committed then there is no power of arrest.

Furthermore, the arrest is only authorised where two further conditions are satisfied:

KEY STATUTE

PACE, section 24A(3), (4)

(3) But the power of arrest is exercisable only if –

   (a) the person making the arrest has reasonable grounds for believing that for any of the reasons mentioned in subsection (4) it is necessary to arrest the person in question; and

   (b) it appears to the person making the arrest that it is not reasonably practicable for a **constable to make it instead.**

(4) The reasons are to prevent the person in question –

   (a) causing physical injury to himself or any other person;

   (b) suffering physical injury;

   (c) causing loss of or damage to property; or

   (d) making off before a constable can assume responsibility for him.

Powers of arrest available to police officers

The additional powers of arrest available to police officers are as follows:

- In relation to *all* offences (not just indictable offences).
- They also apply to anyone *about to* commit an offence (or anyone whom the officer has reasonable grounds to suspect is about to commit an offence).
- Whereas the powers of arrest available to the general public apply only where an actual offence is committed, a police officer can arrest when they *reasonably believe* that an offence has been committed. In such cases, the officer can arrest anyone they reasonably suspect to have committed the offence.

In addition, the officer can only make an arrest when it is necessary for one of the reasons specified in section 24(5).

KEY STATUTE

PACE, section 24

(5) The reasons are –

   (a) to enable the name of the person in question to be ascertained (in the case where the constable does not know, and cannot readily ascertain, the person's name, or has reasonable grounds for doubting whether a name given by the person as his name is his real name);

   (b) correspondingly as regards the person's address; ▶

(c) to prevent the person in question –

    (i)   causing physical injury to himself or any other person;

    (ii) suffering physical injury;

    (iii) causing loss of or damage to property;

    (iv) committing an offence against public decency (subject to subsection (6)); or

    (v) causing an unlawful obstruction of the highway;

(d) to protect a child or other vulnerable person from the person in question;

(e) to allow the prompt and effective investigation of the offence or of the conduct of the person in question;

(f) to prevent any prosecution for the offence from being hindered by the disappearance of the person in question.

KEY CASE

Hayes v *Chief Constable of Merseyside* **[2011] EWCA Civ 911 (CA)**

Concerning: powers of arrest

Facts

A police constable contacted the claimant, saying that he needed to speak to him in relation to an alleged assault. On meeting the constable, the claimant was arrested; however, it was soon decided that he should not be charged and he was released. The claimant instigated proceedings against the police for wrongful arrest and unlawful detention, asserting that the constable had not actively considered possible alternatives to arrest but had simply formed the view that arrest was necessary.

Legal principle

In dismissing the claim, it was held that an arresting officer needed to show: first, that he had reasonable grounds for suspecting that an offence had been committed and that the claimant was guilty of it; and, secondly, that he had reasonable grounds for believing that it was necessary to arrest the person to allow the prompt and effective investigation of the offence. There was no requirement to consider all possible alternatives to arrest. Hughes LJ: 'That also seems to me to be clearly the conclusion which best represents the balance which the law must strike in this area between practicable policing and the preservation of the liberty of the subject.'

KEY CASE

Walker v *Commissioner of Police of the Metropolis* [2015] 1 WLR 312 (CA)

Concerning: arrest and unlawful detention

Facts

Police officers were called to investigate a complaint that the claimant had hit his girlfriend at her house. When they arrived, the claimant was aggressive and threatening. One of the officers told him to calm down or he would be arrested and stood in the front doorway of the house in such a way as to prevent the claimant from leaving, thus detaining him for a few seconds without touching him. The claimant had continued to be aggressive and pushed the officer, at which point he was arrested, with 'public order' being given as the reason for the arrest. A claim for false imprisonment was dismissed because the judge concluded that the claimant's detention in the doorway had not been unlawful as it had been brief and trivial and had not in the true sense deprived him of his liberty. The claimant appealed.

Legal principle

Held: allowing the appeal in part. Since it was not acceptable for an ordinary citizen to interfere with a person's liberty by confining him in a doorway, it was unlawful for a police constable, not exercising a power of arrest, to detain a person in that way. Such detention amounted to false imprisonment. Therefore, the claimant had been unlawfully imprisoned by the police officer for a brief period and was entitled to nominal damages. Sir Bernard Rix (citing Goff LJ in *Collins* v *Wilcock* [1984] 1 WLR 1172): 'excepting the lawful exercise of his power of arrest, the lawfulness of a police officer's conduct is judged by the same criteria as are applied to the conduct of any ordinary citizen of this country'.

Notification of arrest

Once arrested, a person should be immediately notified that they are under arrest and of the reasons for the arrest. Failure to do so may render the arrest unlawful.

KEY STATUTE

PACE, section 28

(1) where a person is arrested, otherwise than by being informed that he is under arrest, the arrest is not lawful unless the person arrested is informed that he is under arrest as soon as is practicable after his arrest. ▶

(2) where a person is arrested by a constable, subsection (1) above applies regardless of whether the fact of the arrest is obvious.

(3) no arrest is lawful unless the person arrested is informed of the ground for the arrest at the time of, or as soon as is practicable after, the arrest.

KEY CASE

Christie v Leachinsky **[1947] AC 573 (HL)**

Concerning: notification of arrest

Facts

Arresting officers failed to notify the arrested person of the reason for his arrest.

Legal principle

Viscount Simon: 'If a policeman arrests without warrant upon reasonable suspicion of felony, or of other crime of a sort which does not require a warrant, he must in ordinary circumstances inform the person arrested of the true ground of arrest. He is not entitled to keep the reason to himself or to give a reason which is not the true reason. In other words a citizen is entitled to know on what charge or on suspicion of what crime he is seized.'

 Make your answer stand out

In discussing the requirements of section 28, cite the comments of Clarke LJ in *Taylor v Chief Constable of Thames Valley Police* [2004] EWCA Civ 858 (CA): 'The question is whether, having regard to all the circumstances of the particular case, the person arrested was told in simple, non-technical language that he could understand, the essential legal and factual grounds for his arrest.'

 Make your answer stand out

In any answer on police powers, be sure to include reference to the Policing and Crime Act 2017 which gives additional powers to police staff who are not fully qualified 'warranted' officers (such as 'community support officers' and 'policing support officers').

Caution

An arrested person must also be cautioned in the following terms on arrest and also when questioned:

KEY STATUTE

PACE, Code of Practice C 10.5

You do not have to say anything. But it may harm your defence if you do not mention when questioned something which you later rely on in court. Anything you do say may be given in evidence.

 Make your answer stand out

The wording of the caution emphasises that a suspect who does not mention information when questioned, but who later seeks to rely on that information as part of their defence in court, may find the court drawing an 'adverse inference' from their failure to provide the information earlier (i.e. concluding that they are lying). This change, which was introduced by the Criminal Justice and Public Order Act 1994, undermines the 'right to silence', which was seen as a fundamental right of the accused. This change was highly criticised and continues to cause argument and concern. See Leng (2001).

■ Search of premises

Search of premises can be either with or without warrant but, in both cases, can only be carried out by a police officer. There is no legal power to search premises available to members of the public.

Search with warrant

KEY STATUTE

PACE, section 8(1)

If on an application made by a constable a justice of the peace is satisfied that there are reasonable grounds for believing –

(a) that [an indictable offence] has been committed; and

(b) that there is material on premises which is likely to be of substantial value (whether by itself or together with other material) to the investigation of the offence; and ▶

(c) that the material is likely to be relevant evidence; and

(d) that it does not consist of or include items subject to legal privilege, excluded material or special procedure material . . .

he may issue a warrant authorising a constable to enter and search the premises.

Search without warrant

The police can enter and search premises without warrant under the following provisions of PACE:

PACE provision	When?
s. 17	To affect an arrest (i.e. enter premises to arrest a person and conduct a search when on the premises).
s. 18	To search premises 'occupied and controlled' by a person under arrest (i.e. once a person has been arrested, to visit and search their house).
s. 32	To search any premises where the arrested person was immediately prior to their arrest (i.e. where a person ran into a house immediately before being arrested and so may have concealed material there).

What can be seized?

KEY STATUTE

PACE, section 19(2), (3)

(2) The constable may seize anything which is on the premises if he has reasonable grounds for believing –

(a) that it has been obtained in consequence of the commission of an offence; and

(b) that it is necessary to seize it in order to prevent it being concealed, lost, damaged, altered or destroyed.

(3) The constable may seize anything which is on the premises if he has reasonable grounds for believing –

(a) that it is evidence in relation to an offence which he is investigating or any other offence; and

(b) that it is necessary to seize it in order to prevent the evidence being concealed, lost, altered or destroyed.

! Don't be tempted to . . .

What can be seized?

Do not make the mistake of writing that the police can only seize property relating to the offence they are investigating. As you can see from section 19, once on the premises, they can seize material relating to *any* offence (even if they did not know about it when they entered the premises). Examiners will frequently include this in scenarios, for example asking whether officers who enter the premises to search for stolen property can lawfully seize any drugs which they find during the conduct of the search. The answer is 'Yes'.

◼ Detention and questioning

The other main area of police powers covers the detention and questioning of suspects. Examination questions usually centre on a number of key areas.

Detention before charge

A key question is how long a suspect can be held by the police without being charged. This period of detention is subject to regular review.

Up to (total maximum hours)	On the authority of
24 hours (subject to periodic review after first six hours and then every nine hours)	Custody Officer
36 hours	Senior Officer (Superintendent or above)
96 hours	Magistrate

Note that the above excludes terrorism cases, where the maximum detention period is currently 14 days.

🖎 **EXAM TIP**

Although not relevant to a problem question on police powers, you might want to mention as part of an essay that there has been a great deal of argument over the maximum period of pre-charge detention for terrorism suspects, with the last government originally proposing to extend the maximum detention time for terrorism suspects from 28 to 42 days. This was defeated in October 2008. Under the coalition ▶

government, the influence of the Liberal Democrats can be seen in the recent reduction of the 28-day limit to the present 14 days under the Protection of Freedoms Act 2012.

Detention after charge

After being charged, the suspect should be brought before a magistrates' court 'as soon as practicable' (PACE, section 40).

Questioning

A suspect may only be questioned in the police station and under caution (see Arrest). PACE also provides for confession evidence to be excluded from court if unfairly obtained.

KEY STATUTE

PACE, section 76(2)

If, in any proceedings where the prosecution proposes to give in evidence a confession made by an accused person, it is represented to the court that the confession was or may have been obtained –

(a) by oppression of the person who made it; or

(b) in consequence of anything said or done which was likely, in the circumstances existing at the time, to render unreliable any confession which might be made by him in consequence thereof,

the court shall not allow the confession to be given in evidence against him except in so far as the prosecution proves to the court beyond reasonable doubt that the confession (notwithstanding that it may be true) was not obtained as aforesaid.

Note that section 76 applies only to confession evidence. By contrast, section 78 applies to any form of unfairly obtained evidence.

KEY STATUTE

PACE, section 78

In any proceedings the court may refuse to allow evidence on which the prosecution proposes to rely to be given if it appears to the court that, having regard to all the circumstances, including the circumstances in which the evidence was obtained, the admission of the evidence would have such an adverse effect on the fairness of the proceedings that the court ought not to admit it.

■ Putting it all together

Answer guidelines

See the problem question at the start of the chapter.

Approaching the question

Consider in turn the stop search and the search of premises. In each case, the central question is whether the officers have acted in accordance with PACE.

Important points to include

- With the stop search, do the officers have the reasonable suspicion required to justify the search? The suspect clearly does not match the description and appears to be stopped purely on the basis of his previous convictions – this is not sufficient.
- The officers do not inform him of their station/names or the object and grounds for the search – another breach of PACE.
- There is the question of whether the barred bus shelter is a place to which the public have access.
- Note that the search extends beyond the removal of outer clothing permitted by PACE 1984 and the Codes of Practice. The officers should not have removed his shirt.
- The officers find items which may be used to commit burglary (one of the specified offences for stop search) but this is 'after the event' – remember the officers should have reasonable grounds to justify the search, not perform the search to produce reasonable grounds.
- With regard to the search of the flat, there is no mention of the suspect being under arrest, which is a requirement of sections 17, 18 and 32. Therefore, the search would be *prima facie* unlawful.
- However, once on the premises, the officers can still seize the drugs and use this as the basis for an arrest.

 Make your answer stand out

Although the search of the flat appears to be unlawful, point out that the pragmatic approach of the courts towards obtaining evidence means that the search would not be challenged by the courts. This is in marked contrast to the USA, where such an illegal search would render any evidence inadmissible.

READ TO IMPRESS

Jason-Lloyd, L. (2006) The new powers of arrest – some food for thought. *Criminal Law*, 160: 4–6.

Leng, R. (2001) Silence pre-trial, reasonable expectations and the normative distortion of fact-finding. *International Journal of Evidence and Proof*, 5: 240.

Newburn, T. and Reiner, R. (2004) From PC Dixon to Dixon plc: policing and police powers since 1954. *Criminal Law Review*, 601–18.

Nicholson, D. (1992) The citizen's duty to assist the police. *Criminal Law Review*, 611–22.

Ormerod, D.C. and Birch, D. (2004) The evolution of the discretionary exclusion of evidence. *Criminal Law Review*, 767–88.

Parpworth, N. (2011) Arrest under PACE – Part 1. *Criminal Law and Justice Weekly* JPN 175: 528.

Parpworth, N. (2011) Arrest under PACE – Part 2. *Criminal Law and Justice Weekly* JPN 175: 543.

Ramage, S. (2006) The revised police PACE Codes of Practice: 'an Englishman's home was his castle'. *Criminal Law*, 159: 6–8.

The Brixton Disorders 10–12 April 1981: Report of an Inquiry (the Scarman Report) (1981). London: HMSO.

Zander, M. (2013) Revision of the PACE codes is nearing completion. *Criminal Law and Justice Weekly*, 177: 583.

www.pearsoned.co.uk/lawexpress

 Go online to access more revision support including quizzes to test your knowledge, sample questions with answer guidelines, printable versions of the topic maps, and more!

Judicial review

Revision checklist

Essential points you should know:

- [ ] The role of judicial review as a mechanism for ensuring the accountability of the executive and as a safeguard against the misuse of delegated powers
- [ ] Decisions which are (and are not) subject to judicial review, and assessing the requirements for bringing an action
- [ ] The various grounds for judicial review
- [ ] Remedies
- [ ] The effectiveness of attempts to exclude judicial review

■ Topic map

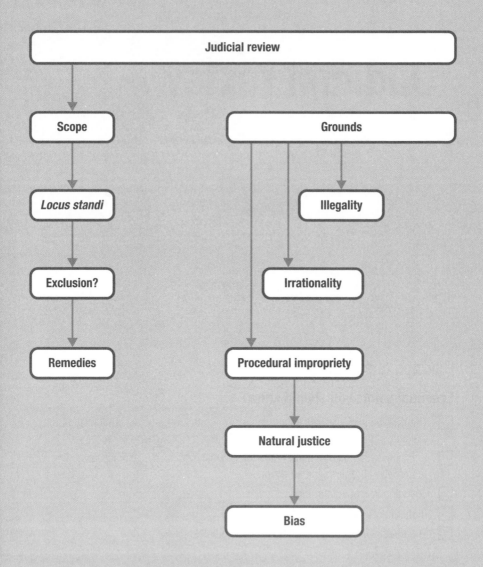

■ Introduction

Judicial review allows the individual to directly challenge at least some of the decision-making powers of the state.

There are relatively few mechanisms by which we can challenge the operation of the state; however, judicial review allows the courts to rule on the legality of decisions made by the state and, in some cases, overturn them. This is a powerful weapon for the individual, ensuring that those in power do not exceed their authority. For this reason, judicial review is an essential topic within any course on constitutional and administrative law and one which is almost certain to feature in examinations in some form or other.

ASSESSMENT ADVICE

Essay questions

Essay questions on judicial review will ask you to consider the two essential elements of any law assessment – *description* and *analysis*. In this way, questions will ask you not only to set out what judicial review is (and the function which it performs within the constitution), but also how effective it is in fulfilling this role. Remember that mere description will never enable you to achieve the higher grades. These are reserved for answers which also display some critical analysis.

Problem questions

Problem questions on judicial review are very common and usually require you to consider one or more case studies to determine which, if any, of the grounds for judicial review may be applicable (together with their likely chances of success). As with all problem questions, the key to high marks is to adopt a methodical approach which deals with each element in turn, weighing up the competing arguments and producing a reasoned conclusion which offers at least some advice to the parties. Remember that you will never have sufficient information to provide unequivocal advice. What the examiner is looking for is an ability to recognise the relevant information in the scenario, and also where additional details are required.

■ Sample question

Could you answer this question? Below is a typical problem question that could arise on this topic. Guidelines on answering the question are included at the end of this chapter, whilst a sample essay question and guidance on tackling it can be found on the companion website.

PROBLEM QUESTION

Alisha applied to her local authority for a licence to serve alcohol at a new restaurant she was in the process of opening. Under the (fictitious) Restaurants Act 2000, a local Licensing Authority may refuse to issue an alcohol licence on grounds specified under section 33 of the Act.

The Licensing Authority meets every month but is also responsible for the licensing of pubs and gambling establishments and so is usually very busy. At the May meeting, the Authority did not have time to deal with Alisha's application and so delegated the task to a sub-committee, made up of three local people, David, Martin and Ian. On the day the sub-committee was supposed to meet to consider applications, David was called away to another meeting and Martin was ill. This left Ian, who made the decision himself not to grant the licence to Alisha.

On 1 June 2007, Alisha received a letter simply stating that her application had been refused. She was not told of the reasons why. She has also been informed that she will have to wait 12 months before she can make a new application.

Alisha has since found out that the restaurant over the road from hers has recently been bought by Ian.

Advise Alisha on whether she might be able to challenge the decision.

■ The operation of judicial review

It is important to recognise that judicial review fulfils a particular function within the constitution in allowing the individual to challenge decisions made by the state. Although that may sound very grand, judicial review is relatively common and is used in relation to many different types of decisions; however, not all decisions made by the state are subject to judicial review. Therefore, when attempting an examination question on the topic, the first point to be established is whether the particular decision is subject to judicial review.

The constitutional significance of judicial review

Judicial review is a mechanism to ensure the accountability of executive power within the constitution. As such, it allows the courts (under certain circumstances) to rule on the legality of how executive powers are exercised and whether they have been exercised in the manner intended.

Any discussion of the role of judicial review allows you to introduce references to a number of different aspects of constitutional law. For example, as judicial review is a mechanism for the judiciary to exert control over the executive, it can be viewed as part of the 'separation of powers'. Similarly, as judicial review is limited to secondary legislation (which is not debated in Parliament), it can be seen to provide a safeguard to ensure that such delegated powers are not misused. Examiners like to see that you are able to link together the various topics in this way.

Judicial review as a challenge to process

It is crucial to note that judicial review is a challenge to the process by which the decision was made, rather than the decision itself. The question is not whether the decision itself was correct, but whether the powers given to the decision-making body were used correctly. Clearly, a party will only seek judicial review when they are unhappy about the original decision, but, nevertheless, this remains an important distinction.

Which decisions are susceptible to judicial review?

As stated previously, not all executive decisions are open to judicial review. To qualify, *all* of the following conditions must be satisfied:

The decision must be made by a public body

As a 'public law' remedy, judicial review is only available where the decision has been made by a public (rather than a private) body.

KEY CASE

R v Disciplinary Committee of the Jockey Club, ex parte Aga Khan [1993] 2 All ER 853 (CA)

Concerning: availability of judicial review

Facts

A horse belonging to the Aga Khan was disqualified from a race by the Disciplinary Committee after failing a drugs test. The Aga Khan sought judicial review of the Committee's decision.

Legal principle

It was held that the Jockey Club was not a public body and, therefore, its decisions were not subject to judicial review. The relationship between the Club and its members was a matter for the private law. Hoffmann LJ: 'I do not think that one should try to patch up the remedies available against domestic bodies by pretending that they are organs of government.'

KEY CASE

R v *Panel on Takeovers and Mergers, ex parte Datafin plc* [1987] QB 815 (CA)

Concerning: availability of judicial review

Facts

The Panel was established by the City of London in order to regulate the takeover and merger of companies. Datafin sought judicial review of a Panel decision to reject a complaint which it had made.

Legal principle

Given the public importance of its role, the Panel could be regarded as a 'public body' and so its decisions could be subject to judicial review. Nicholls LJ: 'given . . . the statutory source of the powers and duties of the Council of the Stock Exchange, the wide-ranging nature and importance of the matters covered by the code, and the public law consequences of non-compliance, the panel is performing a public duty in prescribing and operating the code'.

The decision must be made under delegated powers

Remember the relationship between **primary** and **secondary legislation** in Chapter 5? The primary legislation (the Act of Parliament) can delegate powers to a person or body to implement secondary legislation (rules, regulations, codes of practice, etc.), which is why such provisions are also known as 'delegated legislation'. This is central to the operation of judicial review, because only decisions made under such delegated powers are open to judicial review. Crucially, primary legislation – i.e. an Act of Parliament – is *not* subject to judicial review.

Bringing an action for judicial review

An action for judicial review is commenced in the High Court but requires permission (formerly known as the 'leave') of the court. In bringing an action, you must satisfy the court of two elements:

- the existence of a *prima facie* case (i.e. that there appears to be a case to answer);
- that the claimant has *locus standi* (i.e. the right to bring the case).

Locus standi

This simply means: do you (rather than someone else) have the right to bring this case? This is usually expressed in terms of having a 'sufficient interest' in the disputed matter. This is intended to prevent frivolous and time-wasting actions from so-called 'vexatious litigants'.

KEY CASE

R v Inland Revenue, ex parte National Federation of Self-employed and Small Businesses **[1982] AC 617 (HL)**

Concerning: locus standi for judicial review

Facts

The Federation sought to challenge the Inland Revenue's procedures for levying taxes on casual workers engaged by Fleet Street newspapers. The Federation argued that their members (who did not benefit from this arrangement) were, therefore, disadvantaged.

Legal principle

It was held by the House of Lords that, as the taxation arrangement did not apply to the individual members of the Federation, the Federation could not bring an action. Lord Roskill: 'it cannot be said that the respondents had a "sufficient interest" to justify their seeking the relief claimed by way of judicial review'.

It may be possible, however, for a claimant to bring an action where they have no direct interest if there is a wider point of public interest to be decided by the action.

KEY CASE

R v HM Inspectorate of Pollution, ex parte Greenpeace (No. 2) **[1994] 4 All ER 329 (QBD)**

Concerning: locus standi for judicial review

Facts

The environmental campaign group Greenpeace sought to bring an action to challenge the policy of discharging toxic waste from the Sellafield nuclear plant into the Irish Sea.

Legal principle

It was held that, although Greenpeace clearly was not directly affected by the policy, the fact that it was an internationally recognised organisation, with access to resources and expertise, meant that it was much better equipped to bring an action than the actual residents affected by the policy. Otton J: 'It seems to me that if I were to deny standing to Greenpeace, those it represents might not have an effective way to bring the issues before the court.'

Note also that there are enduring concerns over the misuse of judicial review, which have resulted in recent reforms to the application process and time limits. See Barrett (2013) and Gordon (2013).

■ Grounds for judicial review

An action must be brought on one or more 'grounds' (reasons), as set out in *Council of Civil Service Unions* v *Minister for the Civil Service* (the 'GCHQ' case). There are only three grounds on which an action may be brought, but note that it is possible to argue that more than one of the grounds apply.

KEY CASE

Council of Civil Service Unions v *Minister for the Civil Service (the 'GCHQ case')* [1985] AC 374 (HL)

Concerning: the grounds for judicial review

Facts

It was decided by the government that workers at the secret Government Communications Headquarters (GCHQ) should not be allowed to join a trade union in case this led to them going on strike. The government altered, by means of prerogative power, the terms of employment of the workers to prohibit union membership. The union sought judicial review of the policy.

Legal principle

It was held by Lord Diplock that there were three grounds for judicial review. 'One can conveniently classify under three heads the grounds upon which administrative action is subject to control by judicial review. The first ground I would call "illegality", the second "irrationality" and the third "procedural impropriety".'

□ REVISION NOTE

Note that this case also appears in Chapter 2, as an example of how the courts have treated prerogative powers. Remember that the union sought to challenge the government's policy against union membership at GCHQ (implemented by prerogative power) by means of judicial review.

---

1 'Illegality'

Although the first ground, 'illegality', would seem to suggest that the body which made the decision has acted against the law, it is better to see this in terms of a decision-maker who has acted *outside their authority*. In this way, the decision is said to be *ultra vires* (beyond powers). This can be contrasted with a decision which is *intra vires* (within powers).

! Don't be tempted to . . .

'Illegality' and *ultra vires*

The concept of 'Illegality' can be a difficult one to grasp, but is easier if you think of it in terms of 'absence of authority'. The manager of a shop has the power to make decisions about what happens in the shop, but cannot walk into the shop next door and issue orders – they have no authority to do so. In the same way, a decision-maker will be given powers to make decisions in a specific area; if they move outside that area, their decisions may be *ultra vires.*

KEY CASE

Attorney General v *Fulham Corporation* [1921] 1 Ch 440 (CH)

Concerning: illegality and ultra vires

Facts

The corporation had a statutory obligation (in an attempt to prevent disease) to provide washhouses for the poor. The authority sought to open a commercial laundry under this power.

Legal principle

It was held that the purpose of the power was to provide washing facilities for the very poorest people within the community. Opening a commercial laundry which would charge money to clean clothes was clearly not within the power and so was *ultra vires.* Sargant J: 'the matter turns on this, whether or not the Council has, either expressly or impliedly, power to conduct the operation which it is conducting. In my judgment, neither expressly nor impliedly, under the Acts on which it relies, has it that power.'

KEY CASE

R v *Richmond upon Thames London Borough Council, ex parte McCarthy & Stone (Developments) Ltd* [1992] 2 AC 48 (HL)

Concerning: illegality and ultra vires

Facts

The council was required to consider planning applications, but also introduced a system of 'informal consultations', for which they charged £25.

Legal principle

The House of Lords held that, although the system of 'informal consultation' with applicants was helpful, there was no power to levy the £25 charge. Therefore, this was *ultra vires.* Lord Lowry: 'The rule is that a charge cannot be made unless the power to charge is given by express words or *by necessary implication.'*

Relevant and irrelevant considerations

A decision may be deemed *ultra vires* if it is made on the basis of factors which are irrelevant or, alternatively, if the decision-maker ignores factors which are relevant.

KEY CASE

R v Port Talbot Borough Council, ex parte Jones [1988] 2 All ER 207 (QB)

Concerning: irrelevant considerations

Facts

A councillor was granted a tenancy on a council house ahead of the waiting list. The council justified the decision on the basis that the councillor needed to live within the borough she represented and needed a house to carry out her work for the council.

Legal principle

It was held that this was an irrelevant factor and so the decision was *ultra vires.* The council should base housing decisions on need and on the waiting list. Nolan J: 'There could hardly be a clearer case of a decision which . . . was based on irrelevant considerations and ignored relevant considerations. To put it more simply, the decision was unfair to others on the housing list and was an abuse of power.'

Unauthorised delegation of powers

Similarly, if the decision-making power is given to a specific body, they do not have the authority to delegate that decision-making power to another person. Under such circumstances, decisions made by the person who acts without authority are *ultra vires.*

KEY CASE

Barnard v *National Dock Labour Board* [1953] 2 QB 18 (CA)

Concerning: unauthorised delegation of powers

Facts

The National Board had the power to discipline its members, but delegated this power to port managers.

Legal principle

It was held that the delegation was unlawful and so any disciplinary powers exercised by the port managers were *ultra vires*. Denning LJ: 'there is nothing in this scheme authorising the board to delegate this function, and it cannot be implied'.

---

2 'Irrationality'

The second ground, 'irrationality', is often described in terms of 'unreasonableness', which is defined in accordance with the decision in *Associated Provincial Picture Houses Ltd* v *Wednesbury Corporation* (1948). This is an extremely important decision, as it underpins the interpretation of the term 'reasonableness' which is so commonly used in legal provisions.

KEY CASE

Associated Provincial Picture Houses Ltd v *Wednesbury Corporation* **[1948] 1 KB 223 (CA)**

Concerning: the reasonableness of a decision

Facts

The local authority had the power to license cinemas to open on Sundays, subject to whatever conditions it thought fit to impose. In considering this application, the authority decided that no person under 15 years should be admitted on a Sunday. The company challenged this decision as unreasonable.

Legal principle

Lord Greene MR: 'It is true to say that, if a decision on a competent matter is so unreasonable that no reasonable authority could ever have come to it, then the courts can interfere.'

! Don't be tempted to . . .

Wednesbury unreasonableness

At first glance, the test for '*Wednesbury* unreasonableness' might appear somewhat confusing. All it means is that, if a reasonable authority *could* (not *would*) have come ▶

to this decision, then it is, by definition 'reasonable'. As you can see, this is a fairly broad category and so makes it more likely than not that the decision will be seen as reasonable. However, don't forget it is still quite possible for a decision to be held unreasonable, depending on the individual circumstances.

KEY CASE

R v Secretary of State for the Home Department, ex parte Brind [1991] 1 AC 696 (HL)

Concerning: unreasonableness

Facts

The government introduced a ban on the TV transmission of any speech by the IRA or Sinn Féin.

Legal principle

It was held that this was not so unreasonable that no reasonable Home Secretary could ever have reached the decision. Therefore, the ban was not unreasonable. Lord Donaldson: 'I am quite unable to hold that the Secretary of State's decision was one which was not fully open to him in the exercise of his judgment. Accordingly, it is not one which should or can be reviewed by the courts.'

KEY CASE

Hall and Co Ltd v Shoreham-by-Sea Urban Development Corporation [1964] 1 All ER 1 (CA)

Concerning: unreasonableness

Facts

Hall & Co were granted planning permission to develop their land, but subject to a condition that they construct, at their own expense, a road to be used by the owners of neighbouring land and the general public.

Legal principle

It was held that this was an unreasonable condition, as it passed the public burden of constructing roads to the individual. Willmer LJ: 'The result would be utterly unreasonable and such as Parliament cannot possibly have intended.'

Make your answer stand out

A related area has been the development of 'proportionality' as a consideration in judicial review – i.e. whether the action proposed was no more than was absolutely necessary to address the problem. This is a concept from European law and it has become particularly significant in relation to the implementation of EU provisions and issues of human rights under the Convention on Human Rights. For discussion of the principle in domestic cases, see Qureshi (2007), and for an outline of the principle see *Lawrence and another v Fen Tigers Ltd and others (No 3) (Secretary of State for Justice and others intervening)* [2015] 1 WLR 3485 (SC) Para. 31. The recent Supreme Court decision in *Pham v Secretary of State for the Home Department* [2015] UKSC 19 (SC) has also prompted suggestions that this consideration may become more prevalent in judicial review generally. See Simm and Arshad (2015).

3 'Procedural impropriety'

The third ground, 'procedural impropriety', has the benefit of being the easiest to recognise. As the name suggests, the basic question is: 'has the correct procedure been followed?' If not, then the decision may be called into question. This is intended to ensure that decision-making bodies follow the necessary steps in reaching their decisions.

❗ Don't be tempted to . . .

Questioning a decision for procedural impropriety

Remember that the fact that the correct procedure was not followed does not automatically mean that the decision itself is wrong, merely that there *may* have been a different outcome. This is in keeping with the general purpose of judicial review, which looks to the way in which the decision was made.

KEY CASE

Agricultural, Horticultural and Forestry Industry Training Board v Aylesbury Mushrooms Ltd [1972] 1 All ER 280 (QB)

Concerning: the nature of procedural impropriety

Facts

The minister was empowered to establish Industrial Training Boards, but, in doing so, was required to consult relevant organisations in the area concerned. The Mushroom Growers

▶

Association (a specialist branch of the National Farmers Union) did not receive the consultation documents and so took no part in the process.

Legal principle

It was held that the order establishing the Board, although valid in relation to the bodies which had been consulted, did not apply in relation to the mushroom growers who had not been consulted. Lord Donaldson: 'The Minister was under a duty to consult the Mushroom Growers Association and failed to do so . . . [therefore] the order has no application to mushroom growers as such.'

KEY CASE

Vale of Glamorgan Borough Council v *Palmer and Bowles* [1983] Crim LR 334 (DC)

Concerning: the nature of procedural impropriety

Facts

The council was empowered to issue tree preservation orders to protect selected trees within the borough. Each order required a plan identifying the relevant tree to be available for public inspection. In this particular case, no such plan was made available.

Legal principle

Webster J: 'the map not having been so deposited, the Order failed to comply with a mandatory requirement of the enabling regulations and was, therefore, invalid'.

Natural justice

Within procedural impropriety there is also a ground for judicial review known as 'natural justice' – i.e. decisions which contravene basic principles of fairness. These include the rule against bias (*nemo judex in causa sua*) and the right to a fair hearing (*audi alteram partem*).

Bias

Where the person hearing the case has a financial interest in the outcome, they are precluded from ruling on the matter.

KEY CASE

Dimes v *Grand Junction Canal* [1852] 3 HL Cas 759 (HL)

Concerning: financial bias

Facts

The Lord Chancellor heard a case involving the Grand Junction Canal Company and found in their favour. It later emerged that he held a shareholding in the company.

Legal principle

It was held that the shareholding raised the question of bias and so invalidated the decision.

The suggestion of bias, however, does not always require a financial interest.

KEY CASE

R v *Bow Street Metropolitan Stipendary Magistrates' Court, ex parte Pinochet Ugarte (No. 2)* [2000] 1 AC 119 (HL)

Concerning: bias

Facts

Former dictator Augusto Pinochet was arrested during a visit to London, pending an extradition request from the Spanish government which wanted him to stand trial for alleged war crimes. The House of Lords was required to consider whether a former head of state enjoyed immunity from extradition.

Legal principle

The House of Lords held that Pinochet did not have immunity; however, it emerged that one of the Law Lords had close links with Amnesty International, which was pressing for the extradition to take place. This raised the possibility of bias and so required the decision to be set aside and the case reheard. Lord Hutton: 'I wish to make it clear that I am making no finding of actual bias against him. But I consider that the links . . . between Lord Hoffmann and Amnesty International . . . were so strong that public confidence in the integrity of the administration of justice would be shaken if his decision were allowed to stand.'

Precisely what constitutes 'bias'?

> **KEY CASE**
>
> *Porter* v *Magill* [2002] 2 AC 357 (HL)
>
> *Concerning: the meaning of 'bias'*
>
> **Facts**
>
> In the 1980s, the Conservative Westminster Council adopted a policy of targeted council house sales (in the belief that owner-occupiers would be more likely to vote Conservative). The question of bias arose in relation to the subsequent investigation by the district auditor.
>
> **Legal principle**
>
> It was held that the appropriate test for bias was 'whether the fair-minded and informed observer, having considered the relevant facts, would conclude that there was a real possibility that the tribunal was biased'.

Right to a fair hearing

> **KEY CASE**
>
> *Ridge* v *Baldwin* [1964] AC 40 (HL)
>
> *Concerning: right to a fair hearing*
>
> **Facts**
>
> R was Chief Constable of Brighton and was charged with conspiracy. He was cleared, but the trial judge was highly critical of his leadership. Following the judge's comments, R was dismissed without a hearing or being allowed to present his case.
>
> **Legal principle**
>
> It was held that the right to a fair hearing required a person to be afforded the opportunity to present their case. Lord Hodson: 'Where the power to be exercised involves a charge made against the person who is dismissed . . . the principles of natural justice have to be observed before the power is exercised.'

Is there a right to be informed of the reasons for the decision?

There is also the question of whether the decision-maker is required to state the reasons for the decision. Although there is no general common law duty requiring reasons to be given, the general trend is towards explaining why the decision was made.

KEY CASE

R v Secretary of State for the Home Department, ex parte Doody [1994] 1 AC 531 (HL)

Concerning: the requirement to provide reasons for decisions

Facts

The applicants were life sentence prisoners whose applications for parole were refused without any reasons being given. They sought disclosure of the reasoning behind the decision.

Legal principle

It was held that, although there remained no general duty to disclose the reasons for decisions, this was contrary to the public interest in such serious matters. Also, where a decision was amenable to judicial review, it was necessary for the applicant to know the reasoning employed by the decision-maker in order to prepare their case. Lord Mustill: 'I would ask simply: is refusal to give reasons fair? I would answer without hesitation that it is not.'

Legitimate expectation

Another potential consideration is the 'legitimate expectation' of an applicant. Initially this principle was confined to a legitimate expectation of some procedural protection, for example, a reasonable expectation that the applicant will be granted a hearing before a decision to deprive them of some benefit or advantage is taken (recognised, *obiter*, in *Schmidt* v *Secretary of State for Home Affairs* [1969] 2 Ch 149).

 Make your answer stand out

In discussing the principle of legitimate expectation, point out that this was a feature of the seminal decision in the 'GCHQ' case (*Council of Civil Service Unions* v *Minister for the Civil Service* [1985] AC 374 (HL)).

More recently the principle has been extended to more substantive legitimate expectations that an individual will be granted or will retain some benefit. In such cases, the expectation must be based on either an express undertaking or arise from past conduct on the part of the public authority.

KEY CASE

R v North and East Devon Health Authority, ex parte Coughlan **[2001] QB 213 (CA)**

Concerning: legitimate expectation

Facts

The applicant, who was tetraplegic following a road accident, was moved from a hospital which the health authority wished to close to an NHS facility for the long-term disabled, which she was assured would be her home for life. Three years later a decision was made to close the facility. Following an application for judicial review, a judge quashed the decision, holding *inter alia* that the applicant and other patients had been given a clear promise that this facility would be their home for life and the health authority had not established an overriding public interest which justified it in breaking that promise. The health authority appealed the decision.

Legal principle

Held: the appeal would be dismissed. Lord Woolf MR: 'We have no hesitation in concluding that the decision to move Miss Coughlan against her will and in breach of the health authority's own promise was in the circumstances unfair. It was unfair because it frustrated her legitimate expectation of having a home for life in [the facility]. There was no overriding public interest which justified it . . . here there was unfairness amounting to an abuse of power by the health authority.'

■ Remedies

When answering a question on judicial review, you should always mention the possible remedies available. Note that the names for some of the remedies have changed (the old titles are included in brackets in the table below).

Remedies	Effect
Quashing order (certiorari)	Overturns the original decision.
Mandatory order (mandamus)	Compels the decision-maker to act in a certain way.
Prohibiting order (prohibition)	Prevents the decision-maker from making a decision which would later be subject to a quashing order.
Injunction	Can be either positive (compelling action) or negative (prohibiting action). As such, they are very much like quashing orders and mandatory orders, but can also be made on an interim (temporary) basis, pending the outcome of the case.
Declaration	A judicial statement of the legal position of the parties.

■ Attempts to exclude judicial review

Often (and understandably), decision-makers would like to remove the possibility of their decisions being challenged by judicial review. However, as a constitutional safeguard, this is not generally seen as desirable. The most obvious way of trying to remove the possibility of judicial review is to exclude such powers in the statute which delegates the decision-making power by means of an 'ouster clause'. Despite such statutory attempts to restrict judicial review, the courts have usually succeeded in adopting an interpretation which permits challenges to continue.

☐ REVISION NOTE

Note that the operation of judicial review can raise a number of the constitutional doctrines outlined in Chapter 3. The judiciary exerting control over the executive by means of judicial review raises aspects of the separation of powers, and attempts by Parliament to exclude judicial review by means of statutory provisions illustrates aspects of parliamentary sovereignty. Make sure to mention that you are aware of this in your discussion of judicial review.

KEY STATUTE

Foreign Compensation Act 1950, section 4

Determinations of the Compensation Commission shall not be called into question in any court of law.

(*Note*: this provision was later removed by the Statute Law (Repeals) Act 1989.)

KEY CASE

Anisminic Ltd v *Foreign Compensation Commission* [1969] 1 All ER 208 (HL)

Concerning: ouster clauses

Facts

The claimants sought to challenge a determination of the Compensation Commission. The Commission sought to rely on section 4(4) of the Foreign Compensation Act 1950 (later repealed) which provided that a determination of the Foreign Compensation Commission 'shall not be called into question in any court of law'.

Legal principle

It was held that the word 'determination' did not exclude the court's power to consider whether the decision was correct *in law* (remembering the difference between judicial review and an appeal). Lord Morris: 'if the determination was "not to be called in question in any court of law" … it could not then even hear argument which suggested that error of law had been made'.

■ Putting it all together

Answer guidelines

See the problem question at the start of the chapter.

Approaching the question

- It is essential to be methodical in approaching such scenarios. Set out the relevant legal principles but also *apply* them to the facts as presented.
- Remember to briefly mention even those grounds which you are not proposing to use and explain why they are not applicable. A brief line indicating that you have at least considered them is better than no mention at all, as no mention leads the examiner to question whether you knew about the other grounds.

Important points to include

- The delegation of the power to consider applications to the sub-committee may be an unauthorised delegation.
- Is the 'one man' committee sufficient – does the committee require a certain number of people to make valid decisions? You do not have this information, but it is an important point to raise as requiring further clarification.
- Possibility of bias, given Ian's purchase of the competing restaurant. This suggests grounds of procedural impropriety, which may also extend to the 'single member' committee and possibly 'natural justice' (bias).
- No reasons given for the decision.

 Make your answer stand out

- Mention the absence of a common law duty to provide reasons for the decision but emphasise the increasing expectation that reasons will be given.
- Remember to emphasise that the mere appearance of bias may be sufficient to overturn the decision.
- Do not ignore the issue of possible remedies. Here the most probable outcome is a quashing order.

READ TO IMPRESS

Barrett, N. (2013) Judicial review changes. 24 6 *Construction Law*, 4(3).

Craig, P. (1999) Competing models of judicial review. *Public Law*, 428–47.

Craig, P. (2001) Constitutional analysis, constitutional principle and judicial review. *Public Law*, 763–80.

Daly, P. (2011) Wednesbury's reason and structure. *Public Law*, 238–59.

Dyke, T. (2011) Judicial review in an age of austerity. *Judicial Review*, 16(1): 202.

Gordon, R. (2013) Judicial review: storm clouds ahead? *Judicial Review*, 18(1): 1–5.

Jowell, J. (1999) Of vires and vacuums: the constitutional context of judicial review. *Public Law*, 448–60.

Qureshi, K. (2007) Under review. *New Law Journal*, 157: 315.

Simm, D. and Arshad, T. (2015) At the core of the law. 165 *New Law Journal*, 7659, 10.

Tremblay, L. (2003) General legitimacy of judicial review and the fundamental basis of constitutional law. *Oxford Journal of Legal Studies*, 23: 525–62.

Tremblay, L. (2005) The legitimacy of judicial review: the limits of dialogue between courts and legislature. *International Journal of Constitutional Law*, 3: 617–48.

Woolf, H. (1998) Judicial review: the tensions between the executive and the judiciary. *Law Quarterly Review*, 114 : 579–93.

www.pearsoned.co.uk/lawexpress

 Go online to access more revision support including quizzes to test your knowledge, sample questions with answer guidelines, printable versions of the topic maps, and more!

10

Tribunals, inquiries and ombudsmen

Revision checklist

Essential points you should know:

- [ ] The range of work undertaken by tribunals and their powers
- [ ] The impact of the Tribunals, Courts and Enforcement Act 2007
- [ ] The function and composition of public inquiries
- [ ] The role of the Parliamentary Commissioner
- [ ] The range of work undertaken by ombudsmen

■ Topic map

```
┌─────────────────────────────────────────────────────────────┐
│              Tribunals, inquiries and ombudsmen               │
└─────────────────────────────────────────────────────────────┘

   ┌──────────┐        ┌──────────┐         ┌──────────────┐
   │ Tribunals│        │ Inquiries│         │  Ombudsmen   │
   └────┬─────┘        └────┬─────┘         └──────┬───────┘
        │                   │                      │
        ▼                   ▼                      ▼
   ┌──────────┐        ┌──────────┐         ┌──────────────┐
   │  Areas   │        │ Statutory│         │ Parliamentary│
   └────┬─────┘        └────┬─────┘         │ Commissioner │
        │                   │               └──────┬───────┘
        ▼                   ▼                      ▼
   ┌──────────┐        ┌──────────────┐    ┌──────────────┐
   │   Role   │        │ Non-statutory│    │    Others    │
   └──────────┘        └──────────────┘    └──────────────┘
```

■ Introduction

Not all matters are settled in the courts – there are a range of other mechanisms available.

Although we tend to think of the courts as the place where disputes are settled, constitutional law has given us a range of alternatives, often under the justification of speed and cost. Tribunals operate in a number of areas and provide relatively speedy and informal decisions. The same cannot be said of inquiries, however, which can be incredibly lengthy and expensive. A third mechanism, the ombudsman, is a relatively recent development. All three processes must be considered and their relative advantages and disadvantages understood.

ASSESSMENT ADVICE

Essay questions

Essay questions may ask you to consider the role played by such alternatives to traditional litigation and their effectiveness in terms of constitutional accountability. This requires a clear understanding of the relative merits of each mechanism and the ability to engage in a rounded analysis which places them within the broader constitutional context.

Problem questions

Problem questions may require you to consider a particular scenario or series of scenarios and allocate them to the appropriate forum (e.g. tribunal or ombudsman). Again, the question will require you to demonstrate that you understand the advantages and disadvantages of the various mechanisms.

■ Sample question

Could you answer this question? Below is a typical essay question that could arise on this topic. Guidelines on answering the question are included at the end of this chapter, whilst a sample problem question and guidance on tackling it can be found on the companion website.

ESSAY QUESTION

'Tribunals, inquiries and ombudsmen make a valuable contribution to ensuring the accountability of the state.'

Discuss.

█ Tribunals

Tribunals operate in many areas of law, where they are designed to settle disputes but without the formality, time and cost of litigation. Most act to hear appeals from decision-making bodies or committees. The Council on Tribunals suggests that tribunals:

- are accessible to all;
- are quick, informal and as cheap as possible;
- provide the right to an oral hearing in public;
- give reasons for their decisions;
- are seen to be independent, impartial and fair to all.

Types of tribunal

There are numerous tribunals covering a wide range of administration and decision-making. Examples include:

Tribunal	Cases heard
Asylum and Immigration Tribunal	Appeals against immigration decisions
Criminal Injuries Compensation Appeals Panel	Appeals against decisions by the Criminal Injuries Compensation Authority
Employment Tribunal	Disputes between employers and employees
Employment Appeal Tribunal	Appeals from the Employment Tribunal
Lands Tribunal	Disputes surrounding compensation following the compulsory purchase of land
Mental Health Review Tribunal	Appeals against detention under the Mental Health Act

Advantages and disadvantages of tribunals

Advantages	Disadvantages
Speed – tribunals are generally much quicker than courts	Credibility – may be seen as lacking the 'weight' of a court

Advantages	Disadvantages
Informality – there is an emphasis on less formal language, procedure, rules of evidence, etc.	Increasing formality – as cases become more complex the emphasis on informality may be sacrificed
Cost – even if legal representation is used, the quicker proceedings mean less cost	Increasing representation – applicants may still choose to instruct legal representatives, thereby undermining cost benefits
Expertise – tribunals are usually staffed by experts in the field and focus on a narrow range of cases	

The Tribunals, Courts and Enforcement Act 2007

The operation of tribunals in England and Wales was subjected to radical reform by the 2007 Act, which created a 'two-tier' tribunals system.

The Chambers in the First Tier are:

- Social Entitlement;
- General Regulatory;
- Health, Education and Social Care;
- Immigration and Asylum;
- Taxation;
- War Pensions and Armed Forces Compensation;
- Property.

The four Upper Tribunal Chambers are:

- Administrative Appeals;
- Lands;
- Tax and Chancery;
- Immigration and Asylum.

The Upper Tribunals constitute a 'Superior Court of Record' dealing with onward appeals and judicial reviews.

Make your answer stand out

The creation of the 'two-tier' tribunals system is the next step from the creation of the Tribunals Service, which brought tribunals under the supervision of a single body. This was in response to the Leggatt Review of 2000. For a discussion of the background and implications of this development, see Langdon-Down (2003).

◼ Public inquiries

If tribunals are intended to be an informal and (relatively) inexpensive means of achieving justice, the same cannot be said for public inquiries, which can be extremely lengthy and very expensive.

Types of inquiry

Inquires can be divided into two categories: statutory and non-statutory inquiries.

Statutory inquiries

The power to hold inquiries may be provided for in an Act of Parliament.

KEY STATUTE

Town and Country Planning Act 1990, section 20

(1) Before deciding whether or not to approve a plan or part of a plan submitted to him under section 18(1), the Secretary of State shall consider any objection to it so far as made in accordance with the regulations.

(2) Where the whole or part of Part II of a unitary development plan is submitted to the Secretary of State under section 18(1) (whether or not the whole or part of Part I is also submitted), then, if any objections have been made to the plan or the relevant part of it as mentioned in subsection (1), before deciding whether to approve it he shall cause a local inquiry or other hearing to be held for the purpose of considering those objections.

Non-statutory inquiries

The other type of inquiry is set up on an individual basis to examine matters of widespread public concern. Usually, these are events such as disasters involving loss of life or national scandals. In each case the inquiry is established by the government under the chairmanship of a senior judge to investigate matters and to restore public confidence by producing a definitive account of the facts. There are currently around ten such inquiries established but yet to report.

Recent public inquiries	Subject
Hutton Inquiry (2004)	Death of Dr David Kelly and Iraq intelligence
Saville Inquiry (opened 1998)	1972 'Bloody Sunday' shootings
Cullen Inquiry (1996)	Dunblane school shootings
Taylor Inquiry (1989)	Hillsborough disaster

Advantages and disadvantages of public inquiries

Advantages	Disadvantages
Depth – issues are examined in minute detail.	Time – inquiries often take years to assemble evidence and produce reports.
Scope – evidence is taken from all relevant parties and experts in the field.	Cost – as an example, the cost of the 'Bloody Sunday' Inquiry is currently estimated at £172 million.
Independence – chaired by a senior judge, the inquiry is independent of government.	Whitewash? – reports may face criticism if they are seen as reluctant to apportion blame.
Findings – inquiries can seek to prevent further disasters by making recommendations and apportioning blame.	
Public confidence – inquiries often serve to restore public confidence.	

 Make your answer stand out

If you are discussing the role of inquiries, a useful example to cite is the recent Leveson Inquiry into culture, practices and ethics of the press, established in the aftermath of the 'phone hacking' scandal. The final report of the inquiry can be found at www.levesoninquiry.org.uk.

You might also mention the delay surrounding the current Chilcot Inquiry into the Iraq war, which has been the subject of much speculation and criticism. Details of the inquiry can be found at www.iraqinquiry.org.uk.

Also, to illustrate your up-to-date knowledge, mention the current inquiry into the Grenfell Tower fire, chaired by Sir Martin Moore-Bick, which opened on 14 September 2017. www.grenfelltowerinquiry.org.uk/

■ Ombudsmen

The third major mechanism for accountability is the most recently introduced. The concept of **ombudsmen** (individuals who would examine the use of government powers as they impact on the individual citizen) was introduced into the UK from Scandinavia in the 1960s. Now there are a number of such ombudsmen in both the public and private sectors. They are often titled 'Commissioner'.

The Parliamentary Commissioner for Administration

The Parliamentary Commissioner investigates complaints received from members of the public. The ombudsman investigates allegations of 'injustice in consequence of maladministration' by government departments.

KEY STATUTE

Parliamentary Commissioner Act 1967, section 5

Matters subject to investigation

(1) Subject to the provisions of this section, the Commissioner may investigate any action taken by or on behalf of a government department or other authority to which this Act applies, being action taken in the exercise of administrative functions of that department or authority, in any case where –

    (a) a written complaint is duly made to a member of the House of Commons by a member of the public who claims to have sustained injustice in consequence of maladministration in connection with the action so taken; and

    (b) the complaint is referred to the Commissioner, with the consent of the person who made it, by a member of that House with a request to conduct an investigation thereon.

The 'MP filter'

As indicated above, although complaints come from members of the public, they must be referred to the Commissioner by an MP and this 'MP filter' has been criticised as acting as a deterrent to genuine complainants. However, suggestions that members of the public should be able to complain to the Commissioner directly have not yet been adopted.

Scope of investigations

Schedule 2 of the Act lists the numerous bodies which are subject to investigation by the Commissioner. Some areas, however, are excluded from consideration. These are set out in Schedule 3 of the Act and include:

■ matters affecting relations between the UK and other governments;

- matters relating to extradition;

- actions taken by the Secretary of State 'for the purposes of investigating crime or of protecting the security of the State';

- actions relating to the conduct of the Criminal Injuries Compensation Board.

'Maladministration'?

Some indication of what constitutes 'maladministration' can be found in Annex A of the Cabinet Office publication *The Ombudsman in Your Files* (Cabinet Office 1997):

- rudeness (though that is a matter of degree);

- unwillingness to treat the complainant as a person with rights;

- refusal to answer reasonable questions;

- neglecting to inform a complainant on request of his or her rights or entitlements;

- knowingly giving advice which is misleading or inadequate;

- ignoring valid advice or overruling considerations which would produce an uncomfortable result for the overruler;

- offering no redress or manifestly disproportionate redress;

- showing bias, whether because of colour, sex, or any other grounds;

- omission to notify those who would thereby lose a right of appeal;

- refusal to inform adequately of the right of appeal;

- faulty procedures;

- failure by management to monitor compliance with adequate procedures;

- cavalier disregard of guidance which is intended to be followed in the interest of equitable treatment of those who use a service;

- partiality;

- failure to mitigate the effects of rigid adherence to the letter of the law where that produces manifestly inequitable treatment.

The Channel Tunnel Rail Link

One high-profile example of the work of the Parliamentary Commissioner surrounded the construction of the Channel Tunnel Rail Link, and, in particular, the government's treatment of properties in Kent considered 'blighted' due to uncertainty as to whether they would be on the route. The Commissioner's report eventually led to the payment of compensation to those homeowners affected by the policy.

Other ombudsmen

Health Service Commissioner	Investigates complaints about NHS trusts.
Local Government Commissioner	Investigates complaints surrounding the operation of local government.
Legal Services Commissioner	Investigates complaints surrounding the provision of legal services in England and Wales.

Advantages and disadvantages of ombudsmen

Advantages	Disadvantages
Independent – not aligned to government and so able to safeguard the individual.	'MP filter' – in relation to the Parliamentary Ombudsman, the requirement for complaints to be received via an MP can prevent legitimate complaints from being investigated.
Access – in a position to obtain the relevant information to investigate complaints thoroughly.	Time – investigations may be slow moving.
Influence – can bring about wide-ranging changes to procedure.	Power? – findings may not be binding on those involved.

■ Putting it all together

Answer guidelines

See the essay question at the start of the chapter.

Approaching the question

- This is a relatively straightforward essay question which simply requires a firm grasp of the various mechanisms, together with the ability to demonstrate some degree of reflection and analysis.

- Adopt a simple structure, but remember to return to the question in your conclusion and offer some opinion of the relative effectiveness of tribunals, inquiries and ombudsmen. Remember, however, that your opinion needs to be expressed in a professional manner.

Important points to include

- Outline the nature of state power and the vital importance of mechanisms of accountability.
- Approach each mechanism in turn, explaining what it is designed to achieve and the circumstances in which it is appropriate.
- List the advantages and disadvantages of each mechanism, reflecting on how well each appears to achieve its stated objective.

 Make your answer stand out

- Take the opportunity to include reference to other mechanisms for state accountability, most notably judicial review. Although this is not the subject of the question, a relatively brief mention will emphasise to the examiner that you see the role of tribunals, inquiries and ombudsmen within a broader context.
- Always utilise examples to support your arguments.

READ TO IMPRESS

Cabinet Office. (1997) *The Ombudsman in Your Files.* London: HMSO.

Editorial. (2006) Reform of Public Service Ombudsman. *Journal of Planning and Environmental Law,* 623.

Kirkham, R. (2005) Auditing by stealth? Special reports and the ombudsman. *Public Law,* 740–48.

Langdon-Down, G. (2003) The future of tribunals: a fair hearing. *Law Society Gazette,* 100.05: 21.

Nobles, R. (2001) Keeping ombudsmen in their place. *Public Law,* 308–28.

Quane, H. (2007) Challenging the report of an independent inquiry under the Human Rights Act. *Public Law,* 529–44.

Seneviratne, M. (2006) A new ombudsman for Wales. *Public Law,* 6–14.

Steele, I. (2004) Judging judicial inquiries. *Public Law,* 738–49.

www.pearsoned.co.uk/lawexpress

 Go online to access more revision support including quizzes to test your knowledge, sample questions with answer guidelines, printable versions of the topic maps, and more!

Brexit

11

Revision checklist

Essential points you should know:

- [ ] The background to the Brexit referendum
- [ ] The debate surrounding Article 50
- [ ] The Great Repeal Bill
- [ ] The impact of Brexit on devolution

■ Topic map

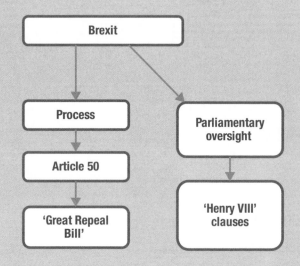

■ Introduction

No single topic is dominating the political and legal agenda like Brexit and that is unlikely to change in the near future.

Although the process of negotiating our exit from the European Union is still in its early stages, it is clear that the process will be far from straightforward and the long-term implications for the UK are equally unclear. What is clear is that few subjects have proved to be so polarising, both for the electorate and the politicians who represent them, revealing historical differences of opinion within both the major political parties. The purpose of this chapter is not to consider the Brexit negotiations themselves, which are fiendishly complex, but instead to highlight some of the background to the current position and a number of the constitutional issues which it raises. With such a fast-moving subject it is possible (perhaps even inevitable) that further significant developments will occur during the course of your studies, but the following should at least equip you to evaluate those events and offer some comment should the topic feature in your assessments.

ASSESSMENT ADVICE

Essay questions

Essay questions may ask you to consider the background to the Brexit vote and the probable constitutional implications for the UK of leaving the EU. Even reaching this early stage in the process has raised a number of significant constitutional issues and examiners may take advantage of this topical debate to test your broader understanding of the relationship between the various organs of state.

Problem questions

Problem questions are likely to be more 'hybrid' questions which may contain a scenario but which then 'ask you to advise X on the constitutional implications of Brexit' and so are really more akin to essay questions.

■ Sample question

Could you answer this question? Below is a typical essay question that could arise on this topic. Guidelines on answering the question are included at the end of this chapter, whilst a sample problem question and guidance on tackling it can be found on the companion website.

> ### ESSAY QUESTION
>
> 'Brexit signals an end to EU law and the return to the sovereignty of the UK parliament.'
> Discuss.

■ Background to Brexit

We saw in Chapter 3 that the European Communities Act 1972 had dramatic implications for the UK legal system and the doctrine of parliamentary sovereignty.

> **KEY STATUTE**
>
> **European Communities Act 1972, section 2**
>
> General implementation of Treaties
>
> (1) All such rights, powers, liabilities, obligations and restrictions from time to time
>   created or arising by or under the Treaties . . . are without further enactment to be
>   given legal effect or used in the United Kingdom shall be recognised and available
>   in law, and be enforced, allowed and followed accordingly
>
> [The reference to 'without further enactment' is crucial, as this means without
> Parliament.]

As mentioned previously, this direct imposition of EU provisions into UK law was most obvious in the case of Regulations which were incorporated into the legal system of the UK without any intervention by the domestic legislature. For many people it was this sense of loss of sovereignty, together with the jurisdiction of the European Court of Justice (ECJ), which caused their resistance to the EU. Another factor in this argument was the expansion of the EU to include more states which would inevitably lead to the greater use of qualified majority voting (QMV) to decide important issues and policies within the EU. To many, this represented an unacceptable restriction on the power of the UK government and Parliament.

For others, the key complaint was levels of immigration into the UK. This included nationals of other EU states who were able to enter the UK under the 'freedom of movement' principles as well as refugees from non-EU states. For others, the perceived restrictions imposed by the European Court of Human Rights (particularly in relation to the deportation of foreign criminals) were the principal cause for concern.

■ The Brexit referendum

The vote on our membership of the EU was held on 23 June 2016 under the provisions of the European Union Referendum Act 2015.

KEY STATUTE

European Union Referendum Act 2015, Section 1

The referendum

(1) A referendum is to be held on whether the United Kingdom should remain a member of the European Union.

(2) The Secretary of State must, by regulations, appoint the day on which the referendum is to be held.

. . . .

(4) The question that is to appear on the ballot papers is—

'Should the United Kingdom remain a member of the European Union or leave the European Union?'

This was the second such vote, the first being held in 1975 (obviously we voted to remain in the European Community at that time). The result was 51.9% voting to leave and 48.1% voting to remain, with a turnout of 72.2% of those people eligible to vote (www.bbc.co.uk/news/politics/eu_referendum/results).

■ Why did we have the referendum?

Both of the main political parties in the UK contain members who are in favour of the EU and those who are against but this division is particularly acute within the Conservative Party, which has, for many years, had a vocal 'Eurosceptic' element – both among Conservative voters and Conservative Members of Parliament.

 Make your answer stand out

Point out that it was the Eurosceptic wing of the Conservative Party which almost caused the fall of their own Prime Minister John Major in 1992, due to their opposition to ratifying the Treaty on European Union (TEU), also known as the 'Maastricht Treaty'.

For this reason, all Conservative leaders have had to deal with calls for a referendum from within their own party but, traditionally, have managed to ignore such requests as all of the other political parties were staunchly in favour of EU membership. However, with the rise of the UK Independence Party (UKIP), Conservative voters who wanted an EU referendum suddenly had a party to vote for which promised to deliver a referendum if elected. The fact that UKIP were highly unlikely to secure enough votes to deliver on this promise did not matter. The danger for the Conservatives was that a UKIP candidate standing in a constituency could split the 'Anti-Labour' vote, thereby allowing Labour to win.

The answer for the Conservatives was to promise a referendum if they won the 2015 general election. The calculation was that Eurosceptic voters who might have defected to UKIP would now vote Conservative on the basis that (unlike UKIP) it was a party which could actually win the election and so deliver on the referendum promise. Remember that from 2010 to 2015 the Conservatives had been part of a coalition government with the Liberal Democrats and, at the time, the most likely outcome of the 2015 election was thought to be another Conservative/ Liberal Democrat coalition. Many suspected that this would have allowed the Conservatives to abandon the referendum pledge as part of the coalition negotiations with the staunchly pro-European Liberal Democrats (much as the Liberal Democrats had done with their election pledge to resist increases in student tuition fees in 2010). Ironically, the problem for the Conservatives came when they unexpectedly won the 2015 election and so were compelled to deliver the promised EU referendum.

 Make your answer stand out

Note that, as in the 1975 referendum, 'collective responsibility' was suspended. This meant that individual ministers did not have to publicly support the government position (which was to remain in the EU) but could express their own views. This also applied to the Labour Shadow Cabinet. For further discussion of ministerial responsibility, see Chapter 4.

After the referendum result, one of the first issues to be decided was when the UK would trigger Article 50, the legal process for leaving the EU.

KEY PROVISIONS

Article 50 Treaty of Lisbon

1. Any Member State may decide to withdraw from the Union in accordance with its own constitutional requirements.

2. A Member State which decides to withdraw shall notify the European Council of its intention. In the light of the guidelines provided by the European Council, the Union shall negotiate and conclude an agreement with that State, setting out the arrangements for its withdrawal.

3. The Treaties shall cease to apply to the State in question from the date of entry into force of the withdrawal agreement or, failing that, two years after the notification referred to in paragraph 2.

The government argued that it could begin this process under prerogative powers (see Chapter 2 but others believed that only Parliament had the constitutional legitimacy to take such a momentous step.

KEY CASE

R (on the application of Miller) v *Secretary of State for Exiting the European Union* **[2017] UKSC 5 (SC).**

Concerning: Article 50

Facts

The Supreme Court was required to consider the steps required as a matter of UK domestic law before the process of leaving the European Union could be initiated. In particular, whether a formal notice of withdrawal can lawfully be given by ministers without prior legislation passed in both Houses of Parliament and assented to by the Queen.

Legal principle

Held. The Supreme Court upheld the decision of the Divisional Court that the government did not have power under the royal prerogative to give notice under Article 50 for the UK to withdraw from the EU. The authority of primary legislation was required before that course could be taken. Lord Neuberger: 'the 1972 Act required ministers not to commit the United Kingdom to any new arrangement, whether it increased or decreased the potential volume and extent of EU law, without first being approved by Parliament... It would scarcely be compatible with those provisions if, in reliance on prerogative powers, ministers could unilaterally withdraw from the EU Treaties, thereby reducing the volume and extent of EU law which takes effect domestically to nil without the need for parliamentary approval.'

As a result, Parliament was required to vote on the proposal and, after impassioned debate, passed the necessary legislation. Although of enormous constitutional importance, the legislation was surprisingly short and the entire Act is reproduced below.

KEY STATUTE

European Union (Notification of Withdrawal) Act 2017

1 Power to notify withdrawal from the EU

(1)   The Prime Minister may notify, under Article 50(2) of the Treaty on European Union, the United Kingdom's intention to withdraw from the EU.

(2)   This section has effect despite any provision made by or under the European Communities Act 1972 or any other enactment. 2 This Act may be cited as the European Union (Notification of Withdrawal) Act 2017.

This enabled the UK to formally trigger Article 50 on 29 March 2017. Under the provisions, this means that negotiations must be completed by 29 March 2019 – the date on which the UK leaves the EU.

■ The 'Great Repeal Bill'

Brexit is not a simple process, especially in relation to the 45 years of UK legislation which is directly affected by our membership of the EU, and one of the principal difficulties facing the UK is how to manage the transition to a new legal framework. The sheer volume of legislation, affecting all aspects of our lives, means that simply repealing all of the statutes is not a realistic proposition. Instead, the government intends to repeal the 1972 European Communities Act and copy all existing EU legislation across into domestic UK law to be addressed on a 'statute by statute' basis in the future. This, it is argued, will ensure a smooth transition.

One of the most contentious aspects of the Bill, however, is the inclusion of so-called 'Henry VIII' clauses, which allow the government to amend primary legislation by means of subordinate legislation without full parliamentary scrutiny. Such powers take their name from the Statute of Proclamations 1539 which gave King Henry VIII power to legislate by proclamation. At the time of writing, the European Union (Withdrawal) Bill has received its second reading.

■ Brexit and devolution

One of the most contentious aspects of the Brexit vote is its impact on the devolution settlement in the UK. This is evident in two key areas.

Firstly, whereas England and Wales voted in favour of leaving the EU, both Scotland and Northern Ireland voted to remain (by 62% and 55.8% respectively). This has led some to question whether Scotland in particular should consider separate EU membership and has strengthened calls for a second referendum on Scottish independence.

Secondly, the position of Northern Ireland has become central to the Brexit negotiations because the Republic of Ireland remains an enthusiastic member of the EU, thereby making the border between North and South, effectively, the border of the EU. For many, the prospect of a 'hard' border between the two states, with checks and customs officials, has echoes of the partition of Ireland which resulted in the violence of 'the troubles'. Conversely, a 'soft' border, with no border controls, is viewed by some as providing an easy route into the UK for economic migrants.

A further complication resulted from the 2017 general election which saw the Conservatives lose their parliamentary majority and retain power only with the support of the Democratic Unionist Party (DUP) in Northern Ireland. It has been suggested that this arrangement breaches the terms of the 'Good Friday' agreement, under which the government undertook to exercise its power in Northern Ireland 'with rigorous impartiality on behalf of all the people in the diversity of their identities and traditions'.

■ Putting it all together

Answer guidelines

See the essay question at the start of the chapter.

Approaching the question

- ■ This is a relatively straightforward question which requires you to have some appreciation of the implications of Brexit.
- ■ Adopt a simple structure, setting out the background to the referendum vote, the intended implications of the decision to leave the EU and the legal obstacles. It is highly unlikely that any examiner would expect you to assess the complex economic implications of the Brexit process and any question is likely to focus on the legal challenges and constitutional ramifications.

Important points to include

- ■ Outline the difficulties with the Brexit vote in terms of the narrow margin and disparities between the vote in England and that in Scotland and Northern Ireland.
- ■ Set out the legal challenges relating to the triggering of Article 50.
- ■ List the features of the 'Great Repeal Bill', not least the use of 'Henry VIII' clauses. ▶

Make your answer stand out

■ Take the opportunity to say something about the historical background to the vote and the degree to which it represented a political gamble for the Conservative Party.

READ TO IMPRESS

Auld, C. (2017) The will of the people. *New Law Journal,* 167(7750): 19.

Cross, M. (2017) News: Lords hit out at 'Henry VIII' powers. *Law Society Gazette,* 11 September, 2(1).

Elliott, M. (2017) The Supreme Court's judgment in Miller: in search of constitutional principle, *Cambridge Law Journal,* 76(2): 257.

Greene, D. (2017) The Brexit Eurostar (Legal World Comment). *New Law Journal,* 167(7755): 6.

Greene, D. (2017) Art 50: a wish list for lawyers. *New Law Journal,* 167(7740): 6.

Reid, C. T. (2017) Brexit and the devolution dynamics. *Environmental Law Review,* 19(1): 3.

Zander, M. (2017) Art 50: the judgment (Pt 1). *New Law Journal,* 167(7732): 18.

Zander, M. (2017) Art 50: the judgment (Pt 2). *New Law Journal,* 167(7733): 18.

www.pearsoned.co.uk/lawexpress

 Go online to access more revision support including quizzes to test your knowledge, sample questions with answer guidelines, printable versions of the topic maps, and more!

And finally, before the exam . . .

Remember that constitutional and administrative law is quite different from the other core subjects typically studied at the same level. Unlike more 'black letter law' subjects, such as contract or tort, constitutional law requires a broader understanding which incorporates elements of politics and history. This can make the subject appear intimidating, but all that is really needed is the ability to place the legal principles within a slightly wider context. Look at some of the examples and tips in this book and don't be afraid to offer an opinion on the various topics in your answers. Providing this is done in a professional, rather than a personal, manner and is supported by reference to some evidence, you will gain credit for producing an answer which is not simply descriptive. As with all law exams, the highest marks are reserved for those students who can *analyse* as well as *describe*.

Check your progress

- [ ] Look at the revision checklists at the start of each chapter. Are you happy that you can now tick them all? If not, go back to the particular chapter and work through the material again. If you are still struggling, seek help from your tutor.

- [ ] Attempt the sample questions in each chapter and check your answers against the guidelines provided.

- [ ] Go online to **www.pearsoned.co.uk/lawexpress** for more hands-on revision help:

  - [ ] Try the **test your knowledge** quizzes and see if you can score full marks for each chapter.

  - [ ] Attempt to answer the **sample questions** for each chapter within the time limit and check your answers against the guidelines provided.

  - [ ] Evaluate sample exam answers in **you be the marker** and see if you can spot their strengths and weaknesses.

  - [ ] Use the **flashcards** to test your recall of the legal principles of the key cases and statutes you've revised and the definitions of important terms.

AND FINALLY, BEFORE THE EXAM . . .

■ Linking it all up

The topic map below highlights the key subject areas throughout the book.

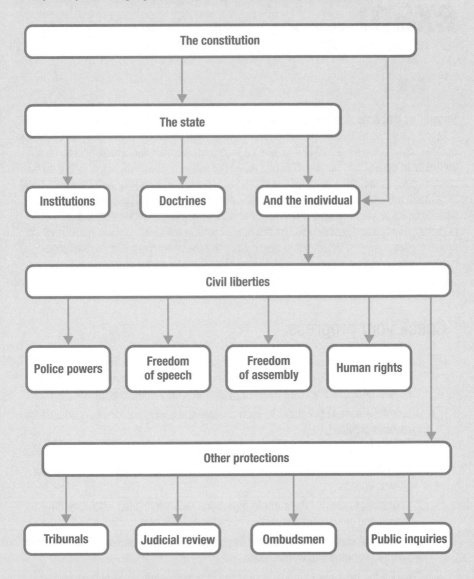

A printable version of this topic map is available from **www.pearsoned.co.uk/lawexpress**

Traditionally, examination questions in constitutional and administrative law tend to concentrate on a single area, rather than combining a number of topics within the same question. However, it is in the nature of the subject that a question on one topic may include reference to another and being able to exploit this within the examination can help you to achieve higher grades. The examiner will want to see that you can approach the subject not as a series of separate areas, but as a whole, and are able to point out where there is an overlap between different aspects of the state. This is particularly common in relation to aspects of the constitution such as the 'constitutional doctrines' of parliamentary sovereignty, the separation of powers and (to a lesser extent) the rule of law. The doctrines impact on all aspects of the operation of the constitution and so questions on topics as diverse as constitutional conventions, royal prerogative, police powers, civil liberties or judicial review should all be answered with some reference to the doctrines of the separation of powers and parliamentary sovereignty.

Check where there are overlaps between subject areas. (You may want to review the 'revision note' boxes throughout this book.) Make a careful note of these, as knowing how one topic can lead into another can increase your marks significantly. Here are some examples:

- ✔ unwritten constitution and the constitutional doctrines;
- ✔ separation of powers and parliamentary sovereignty;
- ✔ constitutional conventions and royal prerogative;
- ✔ police powers and civil liberties (especially freedom of expression);
- ✔ separation of powers and judicial review.

■ Knowing your cases

Make sure you know how to use relevant case law in your answers. Use the table below to focus your revision of the key cases in each topic. To review the details of these cases, refer back to the particular chapter.

Key case	How to use	Related topics
Chapter 1 – The constitution of the UK		
No relevant cases		
Chapter 2 – Where does the constitution come from?		
Thoburn v *Sunderland City Council*	Defining constitutional sources	Supremacy of EU law

▶

Key case	How to use	Related topics
Chapter 2 – Where does the constitution come from? *Continued*		
Entick v *Carrington*	To show that the state must act under legal authority	Civil liberties and the rule of law
Duport Steel v *Sirs*	Illustrates the relationship between Parliament and the courts	Separation of powers and parliamentary sovereignty
Congreve v *Home Office*	Demonstrates that the government can only levy taxes which have been approved by Parliament	Separation of powers and parliamentary sovereignty
BBC v *Johns*	States that there can be no new prerogative powers created	Royal prerogative and parliamentary sovereignty
Malone v *Met Police Commissioner*	States that telephone tapping was legal in the absence of an express prohibition on such conduct	Rule of law and civil liberties/human rights
Attorney General v *De Keyser's Royal Hotel*	Demonstrated that Parliament can overturn any decision of the courts by means of legislation	Parliamentary sovereignty, separation of powers
Gouriet v *Union of Post Office Workers*	Illustrated the non-justiciability of prerogative powers	Royal prerogative, separation of powers
The '*GCHQ*' case	Established that prerogative powers were, in fact, justiciable	Royal prerogative, separation of powers
Ex parte Northumbria Police Authority	Demonstrated that the Sec. of State retained prerogative powers to protect the 'peace of the realm'	Royal prerogative, separation of powers
Ex parte Everett	Established that the state retained a prerogative power to issue passports but that this power was justiciable	Royal prerogative, separation of powers

Key case	How to use	Related topics
Chapter 2 – Where does the constitution come from? *Continued*		
Ex parte Bentley	To show that the court could review the prerogative of mercy	Royal prerogative, separation of powers
Ex parte Rees-Mogg	To demonstrate that the prerogative power to enter into treaties remained non-justiciable	Royal prerogative, separation of powers
Chapter 3 – Basic principles of the constitution		
M v *Home Office*	To show that a minister could be found to be in contempt of court	Rule of law, separation of powers
Ex parte Anderson	To illustrate that it was for the courts and not ministers to set minimum terms for life sentence prisoners	Separation of powers
Ex parte Fire Brigades Union	To demonstrate that when an Act of Parliament allowed a minister to decide when the provisions should come into force, this was not the same as allowing the minister to ignore the Act altogether	Rule of law, parliamentary sovereignty
Entick v *Carrington*	To show that the state must act under legal authority	Civil liberties, rule of law
Jackson v *Attorney General*	To demonstrate the operation of the Parliament Act 1911	Parliamentary sovereignty
Antoine v *Sharma*	Rule of law	Separation of powers
Vauxhall Estates v *Liverpool Corpn*	Illustrated the doctrine of implied repeal – a later statute would override earlier conflicting provisions	Parliamentary sovereignty

▶

Key case	How to use	Related topics
Chapter 3 – Basic principles of the constitution *Continued*		
British Railways Board v *Pickin*	To show that it was not open to the courts to challenge an Act of Parliament	Parliamentary sovereignty, separation of powers
Ex parte Factortame	To demonstrate that, where there was conflict between domestic and EU provisions, EU law will prevail	Parliamentary sovereignty, separation of powers
Francovich v *Italy*	Established that an individual could claim against their state for non-implementation of EU directives	Parliamentary sovereignty, separation of powers
Ex parte Simms	Parliamentary sovereignty	Civil liberties
Chapter 4 – Institutions of state 1		
R v *New Statesman ex parte DPP*	Held that an attack on the integrity of a sitting judge constituted contempt of court	Contempt of court
Morris v *Crown Office*	Held that disruptive behaviour in court constituted contempt	Contempt of court
Sunday Times v *UK*	Identified confusion over the UK law in relation to publications and contempt of court	Contempt of court, EU law
Attorney General v *Hawkins*; *Attorney General* v *Liddle*	Contempt of court	Privacy
Attorney General v *Dallas*	Contempt of court	Juries
Chapter 5 – Institutions of state 2		
Bradlaugh v *Gossett*	Held that the courts had no jurisdiction within the House of Commons	Parliamentary privilege, rule of law, separation of powers

Key case	How to use	Related topics
Chapter 5 – Institutions of state 2 *Continued*		
Ex parte Herbert	Held that the courts had no jurisdiction within the House of Commons	Parliamentary privilege, rule of law, separation of powers
Dillon v *Balfour*	Held that parliamentary privilege protected members from actions for slander	Parliamentary privilege, rule of law, separation of powers
Rivlin v *Bilainkin*	Established that matters which were personal in nature could not be viewed as 'proceedings in Parliament'	Parliamentary privilege, rule of law, separation of powers
The 'Strauss case'	Indicated some of the confusion surrounding the definition of 'proceedings in Parliament'	Parliamentary privilege, rule of law, separation of powers
Makudi v *Baron Triesman*	Illustrates the extent of parliamentary privilege	Parliamentary privilege, freedom of expression
Chapter 6 – Civil liberties and human rights		
Malone v *Met Police Commissioner*	States that telephone tapping was legal in the absence of an express prohibition on such conduct	Rule of law and civil liberties/human rights
Malone v *UK*	The ECtHR held that the telephone-tapping powers in the UK did contravene Article 8, as they were not subject to clear and accountable legal procedures	Rule of law and civil liberties/human rights
R v *LN & E Region Mental Health Review Tribunal*	Established that requiring a person to prove that their detention was no longer necessary infringed their Article 5 rights	Rule of law, civil liberties/human rights, ECHR

▶

Key case	How to use	Related topics
Chapter 6 – Civil liberties and human rights *Continued*		
Wilson v *First County Trust*	Held that a bar on enforcement was an infringement of the right to a fair trial and the right to protection of property	Rule of law, civil liberties/ human rights, ECHR
Wright v *Sec. of State for Health*	Held that a listing of employees as unsuitable without prompt hearings was incompatible with Convention rights	Rule of law, civil liberties/ human rights, ECHR
R (F) (a child) v *Sec. of State for Home Department*	Declaration of incompatibility	Article 8
Benkharbouche and another v *Embassy of the Republic of Sudan*	Declaration of incompatability	The 'reading down' of legislation
Campbell v *Mirror Group Newspapers*	Held that the privacy of model Naomi Campbell had been infringed	Rule of law, civil liberties/ human rights, ECHR
Douglas v *Hello Ltd*	Held that there had been a breach of confidence in the unauthorised publication of wedding pictures	Rule of law, civil liberties/ human rights, ECHR
HRH Prince of Wales v *Associated Newspapers*	Held that there had been a breach of confidence in the unauthorised publication of the diary of the Prince of Wales	Rule of law, civil liberties/ human rights, ECHR
Mosley v *UK*	Held that there was no breach of Article 8 rights by the UK authorities in failing to require the *News of the World* to notify an individual in advance of publication of details about his private life	Rule of law, civil liberties/ human rights, ECHR

Key case	How to use	Related topics
Chapter 7 – Freedom of expression and assembly		
Gough v *United Kingdom*	Defined the scope of freedom of expression and considered the role of the state	Human rights, ECHR
DPP v *Whyte*	Defined the scope of 'tend to deprave and corrupt' under the Obscene Publications Act 1959	Freedom of speech
Calder Publications v *Powell*	Defined the scope of 'tend to deprave and corrupt' under the Obscene Publications Act 1959	Freedom of speech
Shaw v *DPP*	Defined the offence of conspiracy to corrupt public morals	Freedom of speech
R v *Gibson*	Defined the offence of conspiracy to outrage public decency	Freedom of speech
R v *Lemon*	The last successful prosecution for blasphemy	Freedom of speech
Ex parte Choudhury	Held that blasphemy only applies to Christianity	Freedom of speech
Sec. of State for Defence v *Guardian Newspapers*	Shows a breach of the Official Secrets Act in leaking details of US missiles being deployed in the UK	Freedom of speech, official secrets
R v *Ponting*	Shows a breach of the Official Secrets Act but jury acquitted on basis of public interest	Freedom of speech, official secrets
Flockhart v *Robinson*	Established the judicial interpretation of the term 'procession'	Freedom of assembly
Chief Constable of Bedfordshire Police v *Golding*	Use of injunction to prevent demonstration	Freedom of assembly

▶

Key case	How to use	Related topics
Chapter 8 – Police powers		
Rice v *Connolly*	Established that members of the public are under no legal duty to assist the police	Police powers, civil liberties
Hayes v *Chief Constable of Merseyside*	Set out the grounds for lawful arrest	Police powers, civil liberties
Walker v *Commissioner of Police for the Metropolis*	Clarified unlawful detention by the police	Police powers, civil liberties
Christie v *Leachinsky*	Established the requirement for a person to be notified of their arrest	Police powers, civil liberties
Chapter 9 – Judicial review		
Ex parte Aga Khan	Established that the Jockey Club was not a public body for the purposes of judicial review	Availability of judicial review
Ex parte Datafin	Established that the Takeover and Mergers Panel was a public body for the purposes of judicial review	Availability of judicial review
Ex parte National Federation of self-employed and Small Businesses	Concerned the question of *locus standi* for the purposes of an application for judicial review	Availability of judicial review
Ex parte Greenpeace	Concerned the question of *locus standi* for the purposes of an application for judicial review	Availability of judicial review
The 'GCHQ' case	Established the grounds for judicial review	Availability of judicial review
Attorney General v *Fulham Corpn*	Example of *ultra vires* action by local authority	Illegality/*ultra vires*

Key case	How to use	Related topics
Chapter 9 – Judicial review *Continued*		
Ex parte McCarthy & Stone	Example of *ultra vires* action by local authority	Illegality/*ultra vires*
Ex parte Jones	Example of irrelevant considerations influencing the decision-maker	Illegality/*ultra vires*
Barnard v *National Dock Labour Board*	Example of unauthorised delegation of powers	Illegality/*ultra vires*
Wednesbury Corpn	Definition of 'reasonableness'	Irrationality/reasonableness
Ex parte Brind	Example of unreasonableness	Irrationality/reasonableness
Hall v *Shoreham UDC*	Example of unreasonableness	Irrationality/reasonableness
The 'Aylesbury Mushroom' case	Illustrates procedural impropriety in failing to consult affected parties	Procedural impropriety
Vale of Glamorgan BC v *Palmer and Bowles*	To show procedural impropriety in failing to make plans available for public inspection	Procedural impropriety
Dimes v *Grand Junction Canal*	To show the possibility of bias on the part of the decision-maker	Bias
Ex parte Pinochet Ugarte	To show the possibility of bias on the part of the decision-maker	Bias
Porter v *Magill*	Established the definition of 'bias'	Bias
Ridge v *Baldwin*	To emphasise the right to a fair hearing	Right to a fair hearing
Ex parte Doody	To set out the circumstances where there existed a requirement to provide reasons for decisions	Right to a fair hearing

▶

AND FINALLY, BEFORE THE EXAM . . .

Key case	How to use	Related topics
Chapter 9 – Judicial review *Continued*		
R v *North and East Devon HA ex parte Coughlan*	Illustrates legitimate expectation as grounds for judicial review	Legitimate expectation, procedural impropriety
Anisminic v *Foreign Compensation Commission*	To show an attempt to utilise an ouster clause to prevent judicial review	Ouster clauses
Chapter 10 – Tribunals, inquiries and ombudsmen		
No relevant cases		
Chapter 11 – Brexit		
R v *Miller*	Challenged the government's intention to trigger Article 50 without the approval of Parliament	Parliamentary sovereignty, executive power

■ Sample question

Below is a problem question that incorporates overlapping areas of the law. See if you can answer this question drawing on your knowledge of the whole subject area. Guidelines on answering this question are included at the end of this section.

PROBLEM QUESTION

Nathan and his friends are opposed to the government's foreign policy, particularly in relation to the Middle East. On Monday, Nathan learns that the Prime Minister will be visiting the Town Hall the next day to launch a new initiative to help the unemployed. Nathan quickly phones his friends and organises a protest march to coincide with the visit.

The following day, Nathan and his friends assemble around the corner from the Town Hall and begin to march, chanting anti-government slogans. However, the police, who are there in force, quickly arrest them. At the local police station, Nathan is not allowed to see a solicitor and is beaten by two police officers until he signs a 'confession' admitting to a conspiracy to kill the Prime Minister.

204

When he appears in court, the case against Nathan quickly collapses due to lack of evidence and Nathan argues that his human rights have been infringed. The trial judge comments that there may well have been a breach of Nathan's right to a fair trial under Article 6 of the European Convention, but adjourns the case for two months to allow the police to prepare their defence. The case attracts a lot of publicity and features on the evening news as a potential embarrassment for the police and the government.

The following week, the judge receives a telephone call from an official at the Home Office. He is told that the Home Secretary thinks that the judge 'would be sensible' to dismiss the case if he wants his career in the judiciary to continue. Outraged, the judge reveals the details of this conversation to the press and there are calls for the Home Secretary to resign. The Home Secretary flatly refuses to resign and indicates that he is prepared to use the royal prerogative to overturn the Human Rights Act 1998 in this case.

Answer guidelines

Approaching the question

- Such questions simply require a methodical approach. Deal with the various topics in turn, remembering to outline the key principles and authorities.
- Always offer some advice to the parties in a 'problem' question. Never just state the principles without suggesting their likely application. You will never have enough information to be categorical but, equally, you need to do more than just say what the relevant law is.

Important points to include

The protesters have not complied with section 11 of the Public Order Act 1986 by giving written notice to the police six clear days prior to the procession.

Nathan's treatment at the police station clearly breaches the provisions of the Police and Criminal Evidence Act 1984 and its Codes of Practice, particularly Code C, covering detention and questioning. He should be allowed access to a solicitor and the circumstances in which his 'confession' is obtained make it likely that it would be excluded as evidence under section 76 and/or section 78 of PACE.

Nathan's right to a fair trial under Article 6 of the European Convention on Human Rights may have been infringed. Under section 6 of the Human Rights Act 1998, 'public authorities' are prohibited from acting in a way which is incompatible with Convention rights. Both the police and the court would qualify as 'public authorities' for the purposes of the 1998 Act.

▶

The telephone call from the Home Office official raises the question of the separation of powers and the executive encroaching on the role of the judiciary.

The call also raises the convention of ministerial responsibility, as the Home Secretary should take responsibility for the actions of his official, particularly as it appears that the Home Secretary was aware of the call.

The threat by the Home Secretary to overrule the Human Rights Act by means of the royal prerogative requires consideration of the scope of prerogative powers. Following *Attorney General* v *De Keyser's Royal Hotel,* statute will always prevail over prerogative power. This raises the question of parliamentary sovereignty and the accepted principle that an Act of Parliament will always take precedence over unwritten, historical powers such as the prerogative.

 Make your answer stand out

Mention that, in relation to the protest, the police should seek to impose the minimum possible restriction on freedom of expression and assembly that is necessary to safeguard public order. Emphasise that the police are required to balance the right to free speech against the interests of the wider community.

With regard to the detention and questioning, demonstrate a wider appreciation of the topic by making clear that the mere fact that there has been a breach of the Codes of Practice will not automatically result in the exclusion of the confession. The breach must be significant and usually requires some element of bad faith on the part of the police. Here, however, there is little doubt that the police have grossly exceeded their powers by physically abusing Nathan.

When discussing the separation of powers and the possibility of the executive taking powers from the judiciary, it is worth mentioning the decision of the European Court of Human Rights in *Thynne, Wilson and Gunnell* v *United Kingdom* (1990) 13 EHRR 666 which resulted in the Home Secretary losing the power to set the length of 'life sentences'. The court ruled that this was a judicial power which should be exercised by judges, not politicians.

Finally, note that the Human Rights Act 1998 is open to repeal as with any other Act of Parliament, although the political implications of this make it highly unlikely that this would happen.

■ Further practice

To test yourself further, try to answer these three questions, which also incorporate overlapping areas of the law. Evaluate your answers using the answer guidelines available on the companion website at **www.pearsoned.co.uk/lawexpress.**

Question 1

The absence of positive, enforceable rights is only one example of how we in the UK are disadvantaged by our unwritten constitution, which is based largely on prerogative powers and constitutional conventions, and which contributes little to the effective operation of the State.

Assess the accuracy of the above statement.

Question 2

Fircombe is a south coast seaside resort represented in Parliament by the fiercely patriotic Sir Rodney Jones, who is also transport minister.

At his constituency surgery, Sir Rodney sees Charlie Roper, owner of Glamcabs, the luxury taxi company which relies heavily for its income on the executives who visit the seafront conference centres which are central to Fircombe's economy. Having recently invested over £500,000 in a new fleet of luxury cars, Charlie is outraged to hear of an impending EU regulation imposing a 900cc maximum on engines in taxis as part of a policy of reducing emissions on environmental grounds. Faced with either selling his new fleet at a loss or paying for a costly engine conversion for each car, Charlie is determined to oppose the policy and is looking to his MP for support.

The following week, at Prime Minister's Questions, Sir Rodney confronts the Prime Minister and asks him to ignore the regulation, although the government has already indicated that it supports the measure on environmental grounds. In response he is told that the UK, as a member state, is obliged to implement EU provisions whatever the reservations of individual Members of Parliament, although the position would have been slightly different had this been a directive rather than a regulation. Later that day, Sir Rodney appears on BBC News and declares that he is far from satisfied by this answer and accuses the Prime Minister of cowardice. 'This is the British Parliament and we are supreme,' says Sir Rodney.

Is Sir Rodney correct and how does his membership of the Cabinet impact on his ability to speak out on this issue?

Question 3

On Tuesday, news leaks out that a forthcoming conference by a right-wing think tank is to be attended by Dr Smith, an outspoken geneticist who has previously advocated the mass forcible sterilisation of the poor and a massive increase in abortion in order to 'make Britain more competitive'. The conference, titled 'Poverty: How Can We Help?', has been scheduled for the following Friday and, although well publicised in advance, both the presence of Dr Smith and the nature of his speech have been kept secret by the organisers in an attempt to prevent any protest.

Mary and Ian are members of a pro-life group bitterly opposed to Dr Smith's views and, on learning of his attendance at the conference, decide to mobilise the rest of their group, some 500 members, and march through the town in protest on the day of the conference.

They have carefully planned their route so that they will pass two clinics which offer abortion counselling (with the intention of 'persuading' any women they encounter at the clinics to reconsider their decision) before arriving at the hotel where the conference is to be held.

Mary and Ian have conducted a number of high-profile campaigns in recent months which have generated considerable local antagonism and have led to them being arrested twice for public order offences.

On Thursday morning Ian telephones Superintendent Swan and informs him of the forthcoming march. Superintendent Swan instinctively suspects there will be trouble on the day, but knows from previous experience that any action he takes will be challenged immediately by Mary and Ian.

Advise Superintendent Swan.

Glossary of terms

The glossary is divided into two parts: key definitions and other useful terms. The key definitions can be found within the chapter in which they occur, as well as in the glossary below. These definitions are the essential terms that you must know and understand in order to prepare for an exam. The additional list of terms provides further definitions of useful terms and phrases which will also help you answer examination and coursework questions effectively. These terms are highlighted in the text as they occur but the definition can only be found here.

■ Key definitions

Constitution	The framework of rules which dictate the way in which power is divided between the various parts of the state, and the relationship between the state and the individual.
Devolution	The process by which power is given (or 'devolved') from Westminster to Scotland, Wales and Northern Ireland, giving them greater control over their own affairs and the power to make their own laws in certain areas. This is not full independence, however, as Westminster retains power over key areas such as defence.
Federal constitution	A constitution which has a division of powers between the central government and the government of individual states or regions.
Monarchical constitution	A constitution based on the historical power of a monarch who acts as head of state and in whose name power is exercised by the government.
Republican constitution	A constitution with an elected president as the head of state who exercises power in the name of the state.
Rights	There is no single definition of the term 'rights', but a number of legal theorists have suggested possible meanings of the

word. One of the most commonly cited definitions comes from Wesley Hohfeld, who divided rights into 'privileges', 'claims', 'powers' and 'immunities'. The sorts of civil liberties which we normally think of when discussing rights would fall into Hohfeld's definition of a 'claim' right – we have a claim against the state to uphold our 'rights'.

Royal prerogative

This was defined by Dicey as 'the residue of discretionary or arbitrary authority . . . legally left in the Hands of the Crown . . . the remaining portion of the Crown's original authority'.

Unitary constitution

A constitution with power concentrated in central government. Local government may exist, but not with the constitutional status of the states under a federal constitution.

Other useful terms

Absolute privilege

Immunity from legal action which is automatic and complete.

Constitutional convention

An unwritten customary rule which dictates how the state will operate in certain circumstances.

Executive

A body which both formulates and implements policies. In constitutional law this term is usually taken to mean the Cabinet.

Judiciary

The courts. In constitutional law this term is usually reserved for the higher courts (i.e. the Supreme Court and formerly the House of Lords).

Legislature

The body which makes legislation – i.e. Parliament.

Ombudsman

Individual empowered to hear complaints about a particular aspect of the operation of the state.

Parliamentary privilege

The collective rights of Parliament as an institution and the individual rights enjoyed by Members of Parliament.

Parliamentary sovereignty

The principle that Parliament is the most powerful of the organs of state and can overrule the executive and the judiciary.

Primary legislation

Acts of Parliament.

Qualified privilege

Immunity from legal action which is not automatic and which depends on certain criteria being fulfilled.

Rule of law

The principle that the law of the land applies equally to all.

Secondary legislation

Statutory Instruments, Codes of Practice.

Select committee   Committee of Parliament which considers the work of a
                        particular government department (e.g. Home Affairs Select
                        Committee).

Separation of powers   Constitutional doctrine which divides powers between the
                            various organs of state to prevent abuse.

Index

Note: **Emboldened** entries refer to those terms appearing in the glossary

Monarch 58–59
  powers 59
  status 59
Monarchical constitution 5
  meaning 5, 209

N
Natural justice
  judicial review 162
Non-statutory inquiries 176
Northern Ireland
  devolution 68–69

O
Obscenity 114–116
  tend to deprave and corrupt 115
Official secrets 117–119
  disclosure 118–119
  offences117–118
Ombudsmen 171–182
  advantages 180
  disadvantages 180
  topic map 172

P
PACE 132–138
  background to 134
  Codes of Practice 133
  obligation to assist police 134
  stop search see Stop search
Parliament 75–88
  admission to take up seat 82
  dissolution of 22
  executive, and 76
  functions 78
  sale of alcohol without licence 82
  scrutiny 80
Parliament and courts
  relationship 20
Parliamentary Commissioner for
      Administration 178–179
  Channel Tunnel Rail Link 179
  maladministration 179
  MP filter 178
  scope of investigations 178–179
Parliamentary privilege 81–86
  collective 81–82

  contempt, and 82
  freedom from arrest 83
  freedom of speech 83–84
  individual 83
  proceedings in Parliament 84–85
  punishments 83
  reporting of statements made in Parliament 85
  statements by third parties 85–86
Parliamentary sovereignty 45–51
  definition 46
  EU law, and 48–51
  Human Rights Act 1998, and 51
  implied repeal 48
  making or unmaking any law 46
  no one can question Parliament's laws 48
  Parliament Acts, and 46–47
  Parliament cannot bind successors 47
  power of court to challenge Parliament 48
  separation of powers, and 45
Passports
  issue of 22
Police
  obligation to assist 134
Police powers 129–148
  PACE see PACE
  questioning 146
  state, and 131
  topic map 130
Prerogative see Royal prerogative
Previous convictions
  stop search, and 136–137
Primary legislation 79–80
Prime Minister 63
  appointment 22, 29
Proceedings in Parliament
  meaning 84–85
Procedural impropriety
  judicial review 161–166
Processions 121
  banning 124
  imposing conditions on 124
Public decency
  conspiracy to outrage 116
Public inquiries 176
  advantages 177
  disadvantages 177
  non-statutory 176